# Tales of the Road

## Essays on a Half Century of Travel

### Written And Illustrated By

### Jerry R. Davis

*To Shirl,*

*Jerry R. Davis*

authorHOUSE™

1663 LIBERTY DRIVE, SUITE 200
BLOOMINGTON, INDIANA 47403
(800) 839-8640
WWW.AUTHORHOUSE.COM

First published by AuthorHouse 08/31/04

ISBN: 1-4184-8719-8 (sc)
ISBN: 1-4184-8720-1 (dj)

Library of Congress Control Number: 2004095491

Printed in the United States of America
Bloomington, Indiana

This book is printed on acid-free paper.

# DEDICATION

I would like to dedicate this book to

my good friend and pen pal


Margaret (Akins) Briggs

# ACKNOWLEDGMENTS

I wish to thank all the people who helped make this book become a reality. JoAn (Palmer) Good gave me the original idea for the subject matter. Betty Skelly and Ron Baldwin proofread the manuscript in its original rough form. Dale Shelby critiqued the illustrations and made many helpful suggestions concerning them.

# TABLE OF CONTENTS

# PROLOGUE

After completing the writing of my first volume, *Home on the Farm: Essays on a Michigan Childhood,* I assumed that would be the end of my book writing career. To my way of thinking there had been only one book in me and that was it. I was content to continue writing short articles and memoir-type vignettes, each of which filled no more than a page or two of text. That seemed to satisfy my need for creativity and I experienced no burning desire to write a second book. Considering those facts one might ask, what series of events led to this second volume. This is the evolution of my second attempt to write a book.

For the past few years I have corresponded regularly with a second cousin, JoAn, who lives near Gladwin in the center part of Michigan's Lower Peninsula. In the course of our writing back and forth, I often described a variety of experiences I had while traveling to different places in the world. JoAn seemed to enjoy those little stories and often suggested that I write a book on my travels. In the past decades I have read many travel books and usually they leave me unimpressed at best because, often, they are slow-moving and sometimes very dull. Consequently, at least for the time being, I gave the suggestion little serious thought.

JoAn, however, did not give up so easily. She brought up the subject regularly and simply wouldn't let me forget the idea. In my answers to her letters, I underplayed her suggestion and, though flattered by her confidence in my writing ability, continued to disregard it. Nonetheless, the small germ of an idea did begin to take shape in my mind. Perhaps, I thought, the book would not need to be the usual dull travelogue. Instead, it might be a group of essays about some of the odd, strange and curious events that I had been involved in during the course of traveling.

With that new idea in mind, I began making a list of possible subjects for the little travel vignettes. With very little effort, and in much less time than I would have expected, the list grew to twenty-one. Maybe, I thought, there actually was a second book in me. What an exciting prospect! In my reverie over the possibility, I recalled what fun I had experienced while writing the essays for the first book and projected that I might be able to look forward to the same elation a second time. The prospect became very intriguing, indeed.

After the ideas for the new book had partially congealed in my mind, I wrote to JoAn and outlined my proposal and, of course, gave her the well-deserved credit for the inspiration. In a trice she wrote back and added fuel to the fire by enthusiastically endorsing the project. With her encouragement, I eagerly sat down to the computer and started writing the first of the essays.

My initial attempt, which did actually become chapter 1 in the completed volume, is called "The Foreigner." The essay describes a few of my madcap foibles on my first trip to Europe as an inexperienced twenty year old college student in 1953. That was my introduction to how a person feels when he is in an alien environment for the first time in his life. The little essay was a real joy to write and brought back many, many memories, both good and bad, from almost exactly fifty years ago. Immediately I sent a copy of the essay to JoAn who approved of it with gusto. At that point I knew for certain that writing the new book was going to be a most satisfying endeavor and I looked forward to the rest of the project with eager anticipation.

Over the course of the next eight months or so, I wrote the additional twenty vignettes that make up the entire volume. Though some were much more difficult to put together than others, they all provided me with an interesting and gratifying time.

When the twenty-one essays were complete, I turned to the task of drawing an illustration to decorate the title page for each of them. That project took another two months and I found it equally as enjoyable as the writing had been. While doing those drawings I noticed something that surprised me somewhat. The illustrations for the second volume were much easier to render and progressed faster than those I did for the first book, *Home on the Farm.* A couple of reasons for that phenomenon come to mind: (1) Prior to doing the drawings for the first volume, I had done little drawing for many years. (2) Most of the illustrations for the second book had subjects that were in more recent history and therefore nearer in memory.

As was true with *Home on the Farm*, *Tales of the Road* is not a chronological story which begins at some point in time and progresses from there to the present. Instead it often jumps from one era to another as it tells about the, at various times, amusing or poignant story of my travels over the past half century. Each of the vignettes may be read as a complete story unto itself without any references to the others. One may choose to peruse all of them or only some, but my hope is that all which are read give pleasure to the reader.

Jerry R. Davis, May 2004
Albuquerque, New Mexico

# CHAPTER 1
# THE FOREIGNER

"Brriinngg, brriinngg!" clamored the bell angrily. "*Verdammten Ouslander*" (damned foreigner)! screamed the German *frau* as she laboriously steered her bicycle around me and pedaled furiously down the road with her skirt and jacket flapping behind her. Unwittingly I had stepped into the *Radweg* or bicycle path which bordered the sidewalk, thus committing a sin of apparently momentous proportions. Somewhat red-faced, I quickly jumped out of the path to avoid any further confrontations with other irate women.

That was my inauspicious introduction to Germany and my first ever experience in the role of "foreigner". A few moments prior to that I had disembarked from the small Swedish ship, the *Karlstad*, and stepped onto the dock at the German port of Bremerhaven after ten days en route crossing the Atlantic from Montreal, Canada. The din caused by the loading and unloading of passengers and freight in the busy port city, the confusion of loudspeakers barking orders in German, and the totally unfamiliar surroundings, all resulted in strong feelings of alienation. At that moment I realized what it felt like to be a foreigner and it was an emotion that I had never previously experienced.

The time was June of 1953 and I was a twenty year old farm boy from Michigan on my first trip abroad. As a junior in college majoring in history, I counted myself very fortunate to have been selected as an exchangee to spend six months living and working with German farm families. In my own naïve way I thought that I had prepared myself well for the new experience. How wrong I was!

During the previous year I had enrolled in a course in German, and though I couldn't actually speak the language, I did have a small understanding of it. In addition, for months I had labored over and practically memorized a German phrase book. Sentences like, *"Mein name is Jerry," "Wo ist die Toilette?," "Wie geht es Ihnen heute?"* and *"Ich habe einen grossen hunger,"* et cetera danced in my head like the storied sugarplums. Surely the combination of understanding German grammar and knowledge of all those helpful phrases would get me by, wouldn't it?

After going through customs, the six of us who were assigned to remain in Germany collected our luggage and met our guide and interpreter, Frau Horst. She welcomed us warmly in English and we were herded into a small bus that was to take us across the city to a youth hostel where we were going to spend the night. My window seat on the bus gave me an excellent view of Bremerhaven and I drank in the ambiance of the quaint old city as we threaded our way through its streets. Most of the buildings were rather small and looked to be quite old. A few of the side streets were still paved with cobblestones: a holdover from the Medieval Era. In direct contrast, however, were a number of taller, more modern buildings that punctuated the skyline and gave the city a delightfully eclectic flavor.

In a short time we arrived at the youth hostel—a rather drab looking two-story building facing a side street. We were ushered inside and told to place our luggage in a small ante room just off the entrance hall. Frau Horst then took a large key from her jacket pocket and locked the storage room. At the time I thought that was just a bit strange, but later learned her reasons for doing so.

Along with my five companions I was directed to a large dining room where about eighty hostel residents from many different countries were noisily enjoying dinner. At the cafeteria line I picked up a tray and began to collect the various food items. When I reached the place where I was to order the hot food, I decided to practice my German language expertise. In a most ingratiating manner I glibly

3

said, "*Guten Abend. Ich wurde Seife bitte mogen.*" I thought that I was saying, "Good evening. I would like to have soup, please." What I actually said was, "Good evening. I would like to have soap, please." I continued smiling at the lady behind the cafeteria counter, fully expecting her to ladle a bowl of soup for me. Instead she gave me a most quizzical look and said, "*Was wollen Sie?*" (What do you want?) Thinking that the lady must be somewhat deaf, I confidently repeated my request in a much louder voice only to be met with another blank stare from her. At that point Frau Horst, who had been listening to the exchange, came to my rescue and told me what I actually had requested. She said that the word for soup was *Souppe*, not *Seife*. Totally abashed after dismally failing my first attempt at speaking German in Germany, I merely pointed to the soup tureen. After receiving a bowl of its contents I made my way as quickly as possible to a table. There I silently ate my dinner and seriously pondered the wisdom of having made application to be part of this exchange program. The soup was delicious, however, and it went a long way toward raising my flagging spirits.

After dinner I was given a pillow, two bed sheets and a blanket and shown to the small cot in the six-person room where I would be spending the night. As it happened I was the only one of our American group in that particular room. Previously Frau Horst had very sternly warned all of us that under no circumstances were we to lose sight of our personal belongings. She added that we should sleep with our clothing, including our shoes, under our pillows.

It seems that most of the residents of the hostel were rather poor students who were traveling across Europe in the least expensive way possible. To augment their incomes many of them stole from other residents, most of whom were equally as poverty stricken as they. At that point, the memory of Frau Horst carefully locking our luggage in the storage room off the entranceway downstairs came to mind. Then I understood the wisdom of her action.

Though my pillow was lumpy because it concealed my shoes, I immediately fell into a fitful sleep. All night long I dreamed that my room companions repeatedly ganged up and stripped me of my few belongings. My pleas in English fell on ears that were deaf to that language. Morning could not come soon enough for me.

According to the old saying, "Hope springs eternal in the human breast," when morning finally did arrive, I greeted it with my usual optimism and eagerly looked forward to what the day would offer. I was only twenty years old at the time and not easily discouraged. With fervent determination I swore that I was going to enjoy the European trip and nothing was going to hinder that enjoyment.

Before we were to meet the farm family that would be our hosts for the first month of our stay, we were to travel from Bremerhaven to the city of Bonn which at that time was the capital of Western Germany. There the United States occupation officials, who actually governed that part of the nation, had planned a two-day orientation program for us. Bonn is situated on the Rhine River about two hundred miles southwest from Bremerhaven. During those post

World War II days, train travel was the best way to get around in Germany so that means of transportation was chosen for us.

After another short bus trip to the downtown section of the city, Frau Horst gave us our train tickets and dropped us off at the enormous Bremerhaven station. There confusion reigned as thousands of passengers milled about, either arriving at or departing from the city. We found ourselves on our own in that melee and realized that we would have to locate and board the correct train out of what seemed like hundreds before it left the station. I had memorized a sentence from my German phrase book that I felt would be most helpful. It was, *"Welches Bahnsteig nach Bonn, bitte?"* (Which platform is for Bonn, please?) I was about to learn one more lesson about what it meant to be a foreigner.

With my ticket clasped firmly in hand and a determined look on my face I approached a uniformed man at the entrance to the station and asked the memorized question. He looked just a trifle dumbfounded but politely answered me, IN FRENCH! Apparently he was a part of the French occupation forces that governed that northern part of Germany. Because my knowledge of his language was even skimpier than my knowledge of German (in fact it was nonexistent), I excused myself in English and sought help from someone else.

Our little group ventured into the station and once inside I located a sign over a doorway which stated, *"Zu den Bahnsteige"* (to the platforms). Surely we were then headed in the right direction.

There I saw another uniformed official, but before I approached him, I carefully noted that across the visor of his hat was the word *"Bahnhof"* (train station). After assuring myself that he was the person who could give me the information I needed, I once again asked my question, *"Welches Bahnsteig nach Bonn, bitte?"* Obviously he understood my inquiry perfectly and smiled broadly before answering. Then he proceeded to give me a very detailed and precise answer which encompassed nearly three minutes of German spoken so rapidly that I understood only a word or two. None of those words made any sense to me in that context. Fortunately, during his long speech he gestured in the direction toward his left. That was the one and only part of his discourse that I understood. I politely said *"Danke schoen"* (Thank you very much) and we headed off to the left.

After what seemed like a very long hike, we passed a gate with a sign that stated, *"Zug nach Bonn."* (train to Bonn). We had made it! We happily hauled our luggage to the first car that we saw with an open door and began to climb aboard.

European passenger cars are arranged somewhat differently from American train cars. They are made up of small six or eight passenger compartments with a door leading to a long narrow hallway along one side of the train car. In contrast American train cars have two seats on either side of a long car with an aisle down the center.

Our group found its way to an empty compartment in the car and stowed our bags on the overhead ledges. We sat down and admired the plush upholstery and expensive looking fixtures while waiting for the train's departure from the station. Our unanimous opinion was that train travel in Germany was going to be very pleasant in such posh surroundings.

The train started moving backward as it slowly pulled away from the gate. It was just underway when the conductor appeared. He was resplendent and very official looking with yards of gold braid decorating his hat and uniform. The conductor politely said, "*Fahrkarten, bitte*" (tickets please.) We showed him the tickets that Frau Horst had given us. He examined them carefully and then he raised his brows and his swarthy face began to redden. "Oh oh," I thought, "<u>Now</u> what is the problem?" Though he spoke no English and we spoke little German, after much explanation and many gestures, he made us realize that we were sitting in a first class car but our tickets were for third class travel. Only then did it dawn on us why the train car was so luxurious.

At the time, German train accommodations were made up of four classes. Each of the different classes had separate cars and descending degrees of comfort and opulence. The long distance trains, such as the one we had boarded, contained only three classes. The shabby fourth class cars were usually relegated to the smaller local trains that traveled between different small towns in rural areas. Later during my visit I often rode the fourth class train cars and found myself seated on a hard wooden bench surrounded by farm people carrying tethered, live chickens in one hand and eating a bread and butter sandwich from the other.

The conductor politely but firmly made it clear that we had to move immediately to one of the third class cars in back. Once again we gathered our luggage and wearily headed down the narrow hallway in the direction toward which he pointed. On the way we passed through several other opulent first class cars, many lesser-appointed second class cars and at last arrived at our lowly destination near the back of the train. There the compartments were cramped cubicles with cheap, badly worn upholstery covering wafer-thin padding on the seats. The space was simply teeming with humanity. With much difficulty we managed to locate seats in several different compartments of the car. German train travel began to take on a much different complexion from that of our initial impression.

After I finally had my luggage stowed and was settled in my seat, I began to take note of the passing landscape that was visible from the compartment window. The huge North German Plain makes up an entire third of the country. The nearly flat area is drained by many rivers flowing through broad, fertile valleys. Much of the nation's best agricultural soil is found there between wide bands of forested lands. We passed irregularly shaped fields of barley, oats, wheat, rye, corn and sugar beets. Both dairy and beef cattle grazed in lush pastures. Plump hogs scavenged about the quaint old farm buildings. Buildings that seemed to hark back to a long ago time in history.

When we reached the Rhine River, the train sped along its eastern side at the base of a high bank. A number of picturesque medieval castles dotted the higher vantage points on both sides of the famous waterway. River traffic was brisk and included many excursion boats and freight haulers.

About twenty-five miles before we reached our destination at Bonn, we passed through the beautiful and historic city of Cologne. Though much of the old city had been destroyed by the Allied bombing raids during World War II, the undamaged twin spires of the magnificent Cologne Cathedral pierced the late afternoon sky and were clearly visible from the train window. They were a proud reminder of Germany's glorious past.

Just as darkness began to settle around it, the train pulled into the Bonn station. After the relative quiet of the train ride the cacophonous sounds of a busy train station once again greeted our ears. The entire structure seemed filled to overflowing with rushing people, scurrying hither and yon and speaking a variety of different languages—none of which was comprehensible to us. We presented a forlorn looking little group as we stood by the train surrounded by our luggage wondering what to do next.

Our confusion was of very short duration. In a little while we were approached by a representative of the American Occupation government who introduced himself as Lieutenant Welles and asked, in English, if we were the American exchangees who had just arrived from Bremerhaven. We were so grateful to hear the familiar language once again that we almost swamped him with expressions of gratitude and with unending questions.

Lieutenant Welles reassured us, answered the questions that he knew the answers for, and then escorted us to a waiting minibus. He explained that we were going to be spending the next few days in orientation sessions and during that time each of us would be staying with an American family in nearby Bad Godesberg, an American enclave just outside of Bonn. He drove us there and one by one we were introduced to our hosts who welcomed us to their homes.

My host family was a young couple named, John and Sharon Cleaver. John was a civilian employee of the Occupation government and Sharon was a housewife with a young son named David. They had been provided a beautiful apartment in a high-rise building with a view of the Rhine River in the distance. They were wonderful hosts and made me feel very welcome during my short stay with them.

The next few days passed quickly while we learned factual information about German agriculture, manufacturing, economics and politics. We were given instructions on what was expected of us as "grass roots" ambassadors and what we could expect in return from the families with whom we were going to be living. We had time to explore the interesting old city of Bonn which we learned was the birthplace of the composer Ludwig van Beethoven. Bonn is located on the west bank of the Rhine River and the *Siebengebirge* (Seven Mountains) serve as a scenic background for it. Prior to World War II the University of Bonn was the city's main claim to fame; however, many changes occurred when it became the capital of the German Federal Republic (West Germany).

During the orientation I learned that the first German farm family that I would be staying with lived in the far northern part of the country—very near the Danish border. They farmed a large acreage near a tiny, rural village called Suderbradup in the province of Schleswig Holestein. Consequently I would have another long train ride returning along the same route I had traveled previously from Bremerhaven. Suderbradup was situated about a hundred miles north of that port city.

By that time I felt as though I was a real veteran of German train travel so I looked forward to the experience. My traveling companions in the crowded third class compartment were very friendly and I was able to practice my fledgling German with them. They seemed to appreciate my feeble attempts with the language and were most helpful. The fact that they were able to understand even some of what I was talking about gave me the reassurance I needed to continue.

During the next six months I came to know the Germans very well. I found that they are a warm and sincere people who freely take strangers into their homes and hearts. I learned to speak their language passably well so communication became less of a problem. With each successive day that passed during those months I felt more and more at home and less and less like a foreigner.

## CHAPTER 2
## A CIRCUITOUS ROUTE HOME

"You want to cover <u>five</u> countries in ten days by railroad?" asked the incredulous travel agent who had been assigned to the four of us. As a matter of fact that is exactly what we did wish to do. When we explained our proposed itinerary in a little more detail the agent then agreed that, though we would be somewhat rushed, the plan was feasible. He then began to make the train and hotel reservations that we would be using for the upcoming trip.

My three traveling companions were Eloise Cooksey from Kentucky, Joan Fisher from Kansas and Carl Brauer from Wisconsin. The date was early in November, 1953, and we, along with two others, had just completed a four-month exchangee experience in Germany where each of us had lived with four different German

15

farm families for a month at a time. A few days earlier we had arrived in Bonn, the capital of West Germany, and had spent the time since then reporting to the American State Department officials about our experiences and impressions of Germany and its rural residents.

Ten days later we were scheduled to meet in Paris with all of the other exchangees who had visited various European countries during the summer. After sightseeing in the French capital for a couple of days we would travel as a group by train to the port city of La Havre on the English Channel and there board the Cunard ocean liner, *The Queen Elizabeth*, for the trip back to the United States.

That ten day interim was to be our free time to travel where we wished. Eloise, Joan, Carl and I had become good friends while living in Germany and we decided that during the free travel time we wanted to take the train south from Bonn, through the Swiss Alps and on south across the northern part of Italy to Milan. We planned to stay a couple of days there and then board a train traveling south and west to the French Riviera on the northern border of the Mediterranean Sea, pass through the tiny country of Monaco and eventually reach Nice, France. After sightseeing there for a couple of days, our plan was to take the train north to Paris and arrive in time for the general group meeting. Though we would actually be traveling through five countries during that time, we would only be making two overnight stopovers before reaching Paris.

The four of us boarded the train at Bonn and soon were enthralled with the marvelous scenery we observed along the way southward. The route followed the Rhine River Gorge through Germany's central highlands passing cities like Koplenz, Heidelberg and Karlsruhe. Beyond Karlsruhe, the gorge widened and became a broad, flat valley. Off to the east we could see the rugged South German Hills and toward the west were the French Alps. Between Stuttgart and the Swiss border the train passed through the Schwarzwald, or "Black Forest" region. Its name comes from the thick forests of fir and spruce trees that cover the mountainsides there. From a distance the mountains really do appear almost black in color.

At Basel, Switzerland, we left the Rhine River and from there our route followed a generally southeastern path through the Jura Mountains, eventually arriving at Bern, the capital of the country. Beyond Bern we entered the picturesque valleys of the rugged and snow-capped Swiss Alps. That region is without a doubt the most beautiful area on the entire European continent. The white-topped mountains appeared almost purple in the distance and were divided by verdant valleys dotted with steep-roofed chalets and Rococo Style churches and cathedrals. Teams of horses and yokes of oxen pulled primitive wagons and carts along the country byways. Because the Alpine terrain was so rugged the railroad passed through a number of tunnels bored into solid rock. We were delighted to experience the marvelous mountain views that erupted before our eyes as we emerged from the long, dark tunnels.

Shortly before crossing the Italian border the mountains gave way to the broad plain of the Po River Valley that encompasses much of northwestern Italy as well as being the site of our next destination, the city of Milan. Milan is the second largest metropolis in Italy, only giving precedence to Rome, the country's capital.

Three points of interest in Milan stand out in my mind from that visit. The first was the lovely Gothic cathedral which is often referred to as "the wedding cake" because it was constructed of white Carrara marble and topped by hundreds of slender spires. The cathedral is the third largest in Europe and was begun in 1385 but not completed until nearly five hundred years later under the rule of Napoleon I. The four of us were fascinated by the structure's fragile and delicate-appearing beauty. Surprisingly our tour group was even allowed to explore the upper regions of the building's interior near the multi-colored rose windows. From high above on a catwalk, we were able to look down at the cross-shaped nave at least a hundred feet below. I was awestruck when I thought of the obvious foresight and intricate engineering talent that had made such a structure possible during the comparatively primitive Medieval Era in history.

Another noteworthy sight we visited in Milan was the Gallery of Victor Emmanuel which was a forerunner of the modern shopping mall. (That was in 1953 and thus it was well before malls became popular in the United States.) The Gallery was a collection of Italy's best shops set in the form of a large cross and covered by a glass roof. Shoppers were able to keep out of the weather as they made their way from store to store. In addition they could have lunch, a snack or a cup of coffee in the brightly lit, glass-covered courtyard area. I sampled my first ever taste of pizza from a food stand in the Gallery. At that time the exchange rate between the Italian lira and the United States dollar was about 3,000 to 1 and I remember noticing price tags for fine clothing topping 1,000,000 lira in the expensive shops of the Gallery.

The third memorable location the four of us visited in Milan was the site of Leonardo da Vinci's painting, "The Last Supper." We found the world renowned objet d'art located in a monastery next to the Church of Santa Maria del Grazie. Da Vinci covered one entire wall of the monastery's dining room with his masterpiece. During our visit we were ushered into a rather dark and apparently windowless chamber where the huge painting dominated the space. At that time it was badly in need of restoration and the colors no longer were vivid or distinct, but its subjects were still recognizable. As a further insult to the painting, a doorway had been cut through at the lower part of its center just below the figure of Christ. In spite of the painting's deplorable condition, the quality of da Vinci's magnificent artistic ability showed through. Little wonder that the famous treasure is the pride of Milan.

A couple of days later we boarded a south-bound train at the huge Milan Railroad Station and began our trip toward the Mediterranean Sea. Our destination was the French Riviera city of Nice. Shortly after leaving Italy behind and entering France we crossed yet another international border and found ourselves in one of the smallest countries in the world, Monaco. Monaco, an ancient principality ruled by Prince Rainier III, is situated on the northern shore of the Mediterranean Sea. Its 23,000 people live on a land area less than two-thirds of a square mile (371 acres) in size. As a comparison our family farm in Michigan was 244 acres in size, thus it comprised a land area of two-thirds that of the entire country of Monaco!

From the windows of the train we could see Monaco's three towns Monte Carlo, Monaco and Fontvieille, perched on terraces rising up from the narrow shoreline. The speeding train took only a very few minutes to pass through the miniscule country and soon we were entering the outskirts of Nice, a Mediterranean Sea port city nestled in the valley of the Paillon River at the foot of the French Alps. Because it is protected from the northern winds by the mountains, the city has mild seasons and is a favorite winter resort and vacation destination for many Europeans.

Though I enjoyed the marvelous view of the deep blue Mediterranean Sea at Nice, it was there I had one of my greatest disappointments while I was in Europe. For years I had heard and read about the wonderful beaches on the French Riviera. They were touted to be the very best in the world. Shortly after we arrived in the city and were settled in our hotel rooms, we donned our swim suits and set out to learn for ourselves just how superior they were.

We walked to the waterfront a few short blocks from the hotel, intending to take a swim and then do some leisurely sunbathing on the beach. Much to our surprise, we found walking on the shore nearly impossible because it was covered with small stones that made every step a misery. What a disappointment! I had been swimming in the Great Lakes on the shores of Lake Michigan and Lake Huron and there the beaches were covered with very fine sand which made walking easy and comfortable. Thinking that perhaps the stony phenomenon existed only in that one particular part of the beach, we walked perhaps a mile in either direction and found it was the same everywhere. We decided that European vacationers must have feet much tougher than ours if they enjoyed beaches with such stony terrain.

During our stay in Nice we took a short bus trip over to the famous gambling casino at Monte Carlo in Monaco. Though we didn't do any gambling it was interesting to rub shoulders with the "high rollers" from all over the world in the splendid opulence of gaming rooms where it was rumored that people gamble away entire fortunes every day.

We began the final leg of our trip to Paris when we boarded a north-bound train a few days later. The rail route between Nice and the French capital is somewhat over 450 miles in length. It follows the Mediterranean coastline toward Marseille and, after leaving the French Alps behind, it veers northward and follows the Rhone-Saone Valley past Lyon. Then it meanders along the Loire River through

21

the cities of Nevers and Orleans where it joins the Seine River on it way to Paris. The Loire Valley crosses a part of the Northern France Plains and is dotted with quaint vineyards, wineries and lovely old Chateaux built by medieval noblemen.

Toward evening we pulled into Paris and my first impressions of the city were seeing two of its most well-known landmarks from the still moving train. The first of those was the Basilica of Sacre Coeur off to the northeast. It is a tall, pure white church erected atop Paris's highest hill, the four hundred foot high Montmartre. My second impression was of the 984 foot tall Eiffel Tower, the symbol of Paris, which can be seen from all parts of the sprawling city. The train snaked its way through the various neighborhoods and eventually entered the Paris Railroad Station; one of the busiest in the world at the time.

After collecting our luggage, we worked our way through the throngs of people and eventually located a taxi to take us to the hotel where we were to meet the other exchangees. During the short ride, the taxi driver managed to scare all of us thoroughly. The streets were extremely busy and the sidewalks and crosswalks were crowded with pedestrians. The cabbie demonstrated no regard for human life as he aimed the taxi toward crowds of people crossing the streets. Speeding toward the pedestrians, he merely honked to warn them of his approach. Fortunately everyone managed to scurry out of his way in time. We made it to the hotel in an agitated and nervous state.

Our days in Paris were filled with adventure. We visited the Eiffel Tower and took the elevator up one of its slanted legs to the top of the structure. At that time visitors were still allowed to view the city from that nearly one thousand foot vantage point. We toured the Louvre Art Museum, visited the Notre Dame Cathedral, walked under the Arc de Triomphe, and viewed the world-renowned Paris Opera House. We shopped in many of the fine department stores, sipped coffee or soft drinks and ate pastry delicacies at little tables in sidewalk cafes. One evening we took in the show at the notoriously risqué Folies Bergere (usually referred to as "The Follies") where scantily-clad dancing girls filled the stage and the aisles, swung from the rafters above and even descended from the ceiling in flower bedecked bird cages. At the Moulin Rouge Nightclub, in the notorious Plas Pigale, I saw my first strip tease performance. Paris was an eye-opening experience for me, a boy from a tiny rural community in Michigan who had only recently celebrated his twenty-first birthday in Germany. The song "How're you gonna keep 'em down on the farm after they've seen Paree?" comes to mind.

Much too soon, according to our thinking, the days in Paris came to an end and we tiredly boarded the train for La Havre on the English Channel. La Havre is the second busiest French seaport, after Marseille, and is just about one hundred twenty-five miles west and slightly north from the French capital. It lies near where the Seine River flows out into the English Channel at the Bay of Seine. The route to La Havre from Paris crosses the rolling Northern

France Plain which has some of the richest farmland in France. The countryside is dotted with small rural villages and picturesque farm buildings.

From the La Havre Train Station we were transported by bus to the harbor where the majestic *Queen Elizabeth* lay moored at a pier. It had been my assumption that we would board the *Elizabeth* in the same way that we had boarded the much smaller *Karlstad* at Montreal, Canada for the trip from North America to Europe. There we had gone up a short gangway and through a door in the side of the ship. To board this ocean liner, however, we entered a building on the pier where our tickets and luggage were processed. Then we were directed to an elevator which took us up several stories. There we found a foyer leading directly into the ship. One could hardly note when we passed from the pier building onto the liner because the transition was so smooth.

Once aboard we were shown to our room where we dropped off our luggage. Then we hurried to the elevators that would take us up the ten stories to the observation deck because we wished to observe the departure from that vantage point. It was a thrilling and festive spectacle. A band was playing, there were people lining the pier yelling "Bon voyage!", "Gute reise!" and "Have a good trip!" to all of us who were crowding the railings along the deck. The longshoremen began casting off the mooring lines and four tiny tugboats sailed into position behind the liner and began towing the behemoth backward out of the berth. When it had cleared the pier, the stern was swung to the left putting the ship in position to move forward from the harbor and into the bay. Then the tugboats went forward and attached huge tow ropes to the front of the ship and began moving it toward the open water of the English Channel. We were on our way!

The *Queen Elizabeth* was similar to a floating city. Aboard were about 2,000 passengers and 1,500 crewmen—that total was larger than the entire population of my hometown in Michigan! The passengers and accommodations were divided into three classes. The largest group was made up of Tourist Class passengers and I was numbered among those. We slept in four-passenger staterooms with a bathroom down the hall that served several staterooms. The next largest group was made up of Cabin Class passengers. They, for the most part, slept in two-passenger cabins with private bathrooms. The "upper crust" travelers were called First Class passengers. They occupied suites with separate drawing rooms, bedrooms and private bathrooms. Most of them even had their own decks where they could sunbathe just outside their drawing rooms. A separate swimming pool served the First Class and another the Cabin Class but the Tourist Class passengers did without.

Separate accommodations such as dining rooms, recreation areas, shops and observation decks were provided for each of the three classes and though there were unmarked doors between the three sections, the policy aboard the liner was that the groups were not to mingle as there were no areas common to all three.

CESEL

In our Tourist Class dining room we were assigned a specific table and only certain times for eating each of our meals. Our table companions were the same for the entire six-day voyage. At our table were my three traveling companions, Eloise, Joan and Carl, in addition to two delightful English women. One of the ladies was a statuesque blond named Elizabeth who probably was in her mid-thirties. The other was an older but no less elegant lady named Margaret.

During the next six days Elizabeth, Margaret and I became good friends and I learned with delight how zany and adventuresome, seemingly staid and dignified, Englishwomen can be. Apparently they recognized in a trice that I was an inexperienced farm boy and so they took me under their experienced tutelage. Their sophistication contrasted greatly with my lack of it but we got along famously. Together we had a marvelous time.

The second day out, after the ship had cleared the English Channel and was well into the Atlantic Ocean, Margaret and Elizabeth asked me if I had ever spent any time in the Cabin and First Class sections of the ship. I replied that I had only seen those areas on a conducted tour I had taken the day before. They asked if I would like to accompany them on our own little tour of exploration. That sounded like an interesting adventure so I agreed immediately. They showed me to the unmarked door leading to the Cabin Class area which I had assumed would be locked. Wrong! We opened it and marched through just as if we belonged there. From then on we spent equally as much time in the Cabin and First Class sections as we did in the Tourist area and became acquainted with a number of those passengers as well. I was amazed at the unlimited verve and panache Margaret and Elizabeth displayed as we rubbed shoulders with the upper crust. I learned a great deal from them about how to act with ease and savoir faire in situations which could be uncomfortable if one were to allow it.

I have no idea why the two ladies took such an interest in me. When compared with them I felt that I had little to offer the relationship but that didn't seem to bother them in the least. During the traditional costume ball held aboard ship they helped me prepare my costume; the three of us attended many of the entertainments together and we danced the nights away at the shipboard nightclub. We even dubbed ourselves "The Three Musketeers." I feel really fortunate that we were assigned the same dining room table because I never would have had such an interesting voyage without them. For several years afterward we carried on a correspondence with one another. By that time I was back at Michigan State and Margaret and Elizabeth had returned to England. Though I met them fifty years ago, I still have a fond place in my heart for those wonderfully adventurous ladies.

The passage across the Atlantic Ocean was a smooth one and early on the morning of the sixth day we sailed into the New York Harbor. The crew had forewarned us that we would have to be up very early in order to watch as we entered the port. Therefore at five a.m., when it was still dark, we were up on the observation deck. The sun still hadn't risen when we passed the Statue Of Liberty, but it was just as beautiful and impressive in silhouette as it would have been in bright sunlight. As viewed from the ship, the thousands of lights in New York's many skyscrapers made the whole city look like a fairyland.

An entire half year had elapsed since I left the United States and though I had numerous adventures and many once-in-a-lifetime experiences, I was extremely eager to be on American soil once again. While we docked I was antsy with anticipation and then could hardly contain myself as we waited in long lines for going through customs before being able to leave the ship. Finally the processing was finished. I was then able to disembark and take a taxi to the airport where I booked the first air flight of my life. A few hours later I flew out of La Guardia Airport (now John F. Kennedy Airport) and winged my way to Detroit. I enjoyed having a window seat and observing the familiar countryside from a different viewpoint than ever before. In a few short hours the plane landed at Willow Run Airport which served all of the Detroit suburban area at that time. Inside the airport terminal I was met by my older brother, Buddy, and soon we were in his car and driving the last leg toward home and family.

# CHAPTER 3
# FLYING OUT OF ROME

The city of Rome seems to have a tenacious type of affection for me. Though I don't believe that cities have the ability to feel such emotions, indications to the contrary do exist. During both of the times that I have visited the Eternal City, events occurred which proved that it was determined not to let me leave its environs.

In 1966, on my second trip to Europe, I spent most of my three week tour visiting various large cities on the continent. First I spent a few days in Copenhagen, the capital of Denmark and then flew to Oslo, the capital of Norway. After enjoying some of the sights and ambiance of Scandinavia, I boarded a plane for Berlin which at the time was still divided into Eastern and Western sectors. My sightseeing there lasted three days after which I flew to Frankfurt in central West Germany. There I rented a car and drove on the Autobahn north to visit a family I had stayed with as an exchangee during my first trip to the continent in 1953.

From Frankfurt I flew south over the snow-capped Alps and on to Rome. During that eleven hundred mile flight I crossed southern Germany, portions of Austria and Switzerland, and much of the length of the peninsula of Italy. The next few days were spent taking in just a small portion of the many sightseeing possibilities found in the wonderful metropolis that is Rome. Among other places of note I visited St. Peter's Basilica, the Sistine Chapel, the Roman Forum, the Coliseum, the Pantheon and the Fountain of Trevi.

My days in the Eternal City passed much too quickly and soon it was time to get on a plane and head for my last destination in Europe—London. Rome is served by the huge Leonardo da Vinci International Airport. The airport is situated on the southwestern Italian border near the Tyrrhenian Sea; thus it is about twenty-five miles from the city's center.

For the air passengers' convenience there is a terminal in downtown Rome. Passengers may purchase their tickets there, and then bide their time in the large waiting room until their assigned bus arrives. Then they are transported out to the airport. Each bus, or group of buses, is given a flight number that corresponds with the airplane's flight number.

I showed my ticket to the lady at the counter. She processed it and gave me a boarding pass. Then she told me to have a seat in the waiting room and my bus flight number would be announced over the loudspeaker. I waited and waited and still waited some more. The number was never called! My plane's departure time was getting uncomfortably near. I was about twenty-five miles away from both the airport and the plane and was beginning to panic. Not knowing just what to do, I re-joined the line of people waiting to speak to the clerk at the counter. At last I reached the head of the line and asked when my bus flight number would be called. Her rather abrupt reply was, "That number was called over an hour ago and the bus left a short time later. It is already at the airport!" I was dumbfounded!

The counter attendant saw my consternation and added in a somewhat kinder but dubious tone of voice, "There is a bus leaving right now. Perhaps it can get you to the airport before your flight leaves. Hurry!" Believe me, I hurried! The bus seemed to take forever as it wound its way through the side streets before reaching the thoroughfare leading to the airport. About twenty minutes later (which seemed like an hour to me) the bus lumbered onto the airport grounds and finally drew to a halt at the terminal entrance. Impatiently I waited my turn to get off and then ran pell-mell toward the gate. Breathlessly I got there just as the attendant was closing the door. I explained the problem to her. The attendant rolled her eyes in frustration and after much deliberation and a short telephone call; she reluctantly unlocked the door to let me through. As I cleared the entrance to the airplane, the outside door slammed shut and I collapsed into my seat while the plane was taxiing away from the gate. We were soon aloft and when we flew over Rome I gazed down at the sprawling city—happy in the knowledge that it had been foiled in its attempt to hold me in its tight embrace.

Rome's other attempt to prevent my departure occurred some twenty-three years later in 1989 when I was ending a driving trip through Europe with my two brothers. These are the events leading to that incident. My younger brother, Dan, taught courses in business for a university based in Louisiana. For most of his career he was under contract with the university to teach American airmen in Europe at U.S. military bases throughout the continent. Each of his courses lasted three months and at its end he would transfer to an air base at another site.

During the early summer in 1989 Dan was teaching at a base northeast of London, England. That session was scheduled to end in June and his next stopover was an installation near Brindisi, Italy. Brindisi was situated near the southeastern tip of the heel of the boot of Italy—nearly two thousand miles, as the crow flies, from London. Dan was reluctant to make the long drive by himself and desired company. He contacted our older brother, Laurel, who lived near Seattle, Washington, and me, a Michigan resident, and asked if we were interested in flying to London and meeting him there.

Dan's plan was that the three of us together would leisurely make the drive from England to Italy during his free month between assignments. We could board the car ferry in England and cross the

North Sea to Belgium, continue driving through the Netherlands, Germany, Austria and finally ending the tour about two weeks later at Brindisi. Later he would take us to Rome where we could catch our flights back to the United States.

It sounded like a good plan to us. My older brother had never been to Europe and it had been many years since I had last visited the continent, so we accepted Dan's proposal with enthusiasm. We both arrived at Heathrow Airport outside London within hours of one another. Dan met us there and we spent a couple of days doing some sightseeing in the vicinity. I remember that we visited Stonehenge just west of London, a bird sanctuary on the North Sea, and several medieval castles in southeastern England.

A few days later we boarded the auto ferry at Southend-on-Sea and sailed to Bruges, Belgium. From there we drove to Ghent before heading north to Amsterdam, in the Netherlands. Our goal was to see the huge tulip fields north of that city. When we found them they were in full bloom and we were awestruck with their size and beauty. The entire landscape seemed to be divided by color! Fields of red tulips abutted fields of yellow ones which lay next to fields of pink ones and so on across the kaleidoscopic terrain.

From the Netherlands we drove southeast toward the German border and soon after crossing it we entered the famous Autobahn and sped south. Drivers can make extremely good time on the Autobahn because it is a four lane divided highway with no speed limit along its length. Our destination was the tiny rural village of

Lich in the province of Hesse. In 1953, while visiting Germany for the first time, I had lived for a time in Lich with a family named Meyer. We intended to visit the family for a short while before continuing southward toward Austria.

The Meyers were surprised but very happy to see us. They greeted us like long lost family members and welcomed us into their home. The fact that they previously had never met either of my brothers made no difference. They insisted that we spend the night with them rather than finding rooms in the nearby hotel as had been our original intention. We all went out for dinner at a local restaurant and spent a very pleasant evening together. The Meyers, especially the children, speak some English but, for the most part, we spoke their language. I was able to practice my German for the first time in a long time and soon learned that I was no longer as fluent as previously. In the morning they fed us breakfast and showed us the way back to the Autobahn and we were once again on our way.

Next we drove to the southern German province of Bavaria where we planned to visit Mad King Ludwig's castle called, Neuschwanstein. Ludwig was referred to as "mad" because during his reign he bankrupted his country by constantly building castle after castle—each more expensive that its predecessor. Neuschwanstein is probably the most impressive of all and it majestically dominates the top of a very steep hill which overlooks a lush, green valley and picturesque lake surrounded by the breathtaking Bavarian

Alps. Ironically, though he spent millions on the magnificent castle, Ludwig only stayed there a very few days.

Early in the evening we crossed the border into Austria and spent the night in a small bed and breakfast nestled in the Austrian Alps. In the morning we drove on to Innsbruck, a city famous for hosting the Winter Olympics. There we rode the Funicular, a steep cable railway, which took us up near the mountaintop where we were able to see a summer glacier and view the city below. We even walked a short distance across a snow-covered plateau. What a glorious view we had of the rugged Alpine countryside from that height!

When our little threesome had been on the road for a week and a half, we crossed the border into Italy, thus leaving the German-speaking countries. Up to that time we had been relying on my German for ordering meals in restaurants and making arrangements for renting rooms at night. Though it was not "textbook" German, it was passable enough to be understood. In direct contrast, however, my knowledge of Italian can be summed up in very few words and they all seemed to have something to do with food or drink. Words such as *pizza, lasagna, pasta, linguini, spaghetti, asti spumonte, vino*, and *lambrusco* came to mind immediately, but few others did. The first major Italian city we planned to visit was Venice but we needed to spend a night on the way to that destination.

Early that evening we pulled into the little city of Belluna and parked in front of an *albergo* (inn) on the main square. Nervously we entered and approached the reception desk where a young lady presided. I asked if she spoke English. "No" was the answer. Then she asked me, "*Sprechen Sie Deutsch*? (Do you speak German?)" "*Jawohl*! (Yes for certain!)" I replied. We were saved! Later she explained that she had spent a year in Germany on an exchange program, therefore had learned the language the same way I did. The young lady was most kind and not only did she see that we were settled comfortably in our rooms, but later assisted us in the dining room at dinner by translating the menu into German. I, in turn, translated the German into English for my brothers.

For the next week we crisscrossed the Italian Peninsula and visited not only Venice, with its canals, but also Pisa, with its leaning tower, and Florence with its *Ponte Vecchio* (Old Bridge). Besides visiting the bridge with its quaint shops, our aim in Florence was to see the original of Michelangelo's famous statue of *David*. After spending hours locating the museum where it was on display, we learned to our dismay that the building was closed for repairs. We had to make do with viewing a poor replica of the statue on the square in front.

Along the eastern coast of the peninsula near the Adriatic Sea, lies one of the smallest countries in the world. San Marino, only 24 square miles in area, is completely surrounded by Italy. Its 18,000 residents are very independent and earn their living from the tourist trade and postage stamps. We drove up the steep, twisty road to the town of San Marino, the capital, which straddles a hill jutting up from the valley floor.

By the week's end we had come to the conclusion of our southward journey at Brindisi. That is a busy Italian port city that looks eastward across the Adriatic Sea toward Albania and Greece.

My brother's apartment looked very welcoming to us after our weeks on the road. We all spent a couple of days for rest and recuperation there. But shortly we were on the way again! This time we were driving to Rome, about four hundred miles straight west from Brindisi. While we were entering the city, I thought back nearly a quarter of a century on my earlier visit to Rome. I recalled the series of events that seemed intent on preventing my departure. To myself I vowed that the same thing would not recur.

We located a *Pensione* (guesthouse) on a small, cluttered side street and made arrangements to spend the night there. I was to fly out of Rome rather early the next day, so it meant that I had to be at the midtown terminal even earlier to catch my bus to the da Vinci Airport outside of the city. The *Pensione* was a long way from the city center and I planned to get there by subway. Therefore I made a practice run that afternoon. All went well and I convinced myself that nothing would prevent me from boarding my plane on time the next day. How naïve I was.

Morning came and it found me up and all packed by 4:00. I bid my brothers goodbye in our room and hurried down to the lobby. There I discovered to my dismay that the front door was locked! No one was on duty at that early hour and I rattled the door in utter frustration. How was I going to get out of the building? I frantically paced back and forth pondering my dilemma. Precious time was passing and I was imprisoned.

Eventually I began to explore the first floor of the establishment. Down a long hallway toward the back of the building was another outside door. Good, it was not locked! After exiting I learned that the door led to an alley running along the side of the *Pensione*. I made a hurried escape and headed in the direction of the subway entrance.

At that hour of the morning the subterranean station area was very quiet and nearly deserted. After walking up to the ticket booth, I was nonplussed to see that it was closed! A sign showing the hands of a clock indicated that it wouldn't open for over two hours! Once again I panicked. Two trains stopped and then resumed their travel (without me aboard) while I stood on the opposite side of the barrier wondering what I was to do. Horrible visions came and went about my still being there when the plane took off for New York City.

A uniformed security guard walked by and I approached him. After learning that he spoke no English, I used all sorts of frantic gestures to let him know about my problem. I pointed at my watch and said, "*Aeroporto* (Airport)," gestured in the direction of the city center, and flapped my arms to indicate the airplane taking off. By that time beads of sweat were running down my face. The guard smiled ruefully and pointed out the turnstile leading through the subway barrier. He didn't see any problem. I let him know that I had no ticket by pointing at the closed booth. Ah, the light of understanding crossed his face. He pointed out the sign indicating when the booth would re-open. With further frantic arm gestures I let him know about the plane's imminent departure. Once again he beamed with comprehension.

The guard held up his arms to let me know that he had no solution for my problem. We stood there looking helplessly at one another as precious time passed. A moment later his eyes opened wide as he thought of a way out of the dilemma. He reached in his wallet and extracted a card. *Then he handed me his own personal pass for the subway.* I murmured "*Grazie, grazie* (Thank you, thank you)," and got out my wallet to pay him for it. He refused the money and instead shook my hand and wished me *Viaggio buono* (Good trip.)

Using the guard's pass I hurried through the turnstile and boarded the next train. When we arrived at the city center I learned that there were two exits out of the subway. They came up on opposite sides of the huge city square. Of course, unknowingly I chose the one that forced me to run the entire length of the square to get to the terminal. Obviously I had chosen the other exit during my "dry run" the previous afternoon.

By the time I belatedly reached the building, the bus had long since left for the airport and I was forced to wait for another. The ride to the airport and the pell-mell rush to the airplane were nearly exact duplicates of those same events that had transpired twenty-three years previously. I made it onto the plane before its departure, but with only a few seconds to spare!

Once again the city of Rome had very nearly kept me in its clutches and prevented my leaving. As we flew out over the Mediterranean Sea and headed toward the Atlantic Ocean, I pondered the strange attraction the city appeared to have for me. Would those same sorts of events occur yet again if I were to visit a third time? That question has never been answered because, to date, I haven't been back.

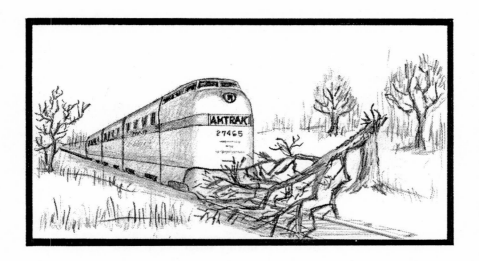

# CHAPTER 4
# ON THE TRAIN TO CHICAGO

If I were seeking excitement-filled adventure, generally I would not look for it aboard the Amtrack train from Michigan to Chicago. I have traveled that route many times during the past few decades and normally it has been a long and somewhat tedious journey. As the train made its way through the rather flat-featured counties of southern Michigan, the rural countryside with its neat farms and small hamlets was pleasant, but it didn't inspire excitement in me on any level. The real stimulation usually came at the end of the trip in the ever vibrant city of Chicago. There I found provocative night life, fine dining, outstanding museums, professional theatre, and unlimited shopping possibilities—all non-existent in my rather mundane home city of Midland, Michigan.

Though most of my Chicago train rides lacked any sort of noteworthiness, there were some excursions that proved to be the exact opposite. They, unlike the rest, have remained in the forefront of my memories in minute detail. Two particular train trips to and from the city stand out as the ones I remember best.

During the late 1980's (probably in 1988) a friend and I decided that we were fed up with our humdrum, unchanging existence during that long and extremely cold winter. We decided to spice up our lives just a bit by spending what we hoped would be an exhilarating weekend in Chicago. We contacted a travel bureau in Midland and booked a package trip that included not only the train fare to and from the city but also accommodations for two nights at the Days Inn on Lakeshore Drive. We looked forward to a couple of fun-filled days in the Windy City.

There is no Amtrack service directly to Midland, therefore we drove sixty miles south to the city of Flint where we boarded the train. Flint, an industrial center of about 300,000 residents, lay on the main east-west railway line crossing Michigan. We could board trains there for traveling either east toward Port Huron and on to Toronto, Canada or west toward Battle Creek and eventually to Chicago.

The train made it usual humdrum and uneventful way across southern Michigan and, just after darkness settled around us, it pulled into downtown Chicago's Union Station. From there we took a taxi to the motel. Though the city was locked in a deepfreeze that weekend we were bothered little by the sub-zero weather as we made the rounds of the city's hot spots and other places of interest. The two days proved to be delightful and in far too short a time Sunday evening arrived. That necessitated our re-boarding the train for the final leg of our weekend jaunt.

We taxied to Union Station, sullenly boarded the train and glumly looked back at the bright lights of downtown Chicago as they receded into the distance. The train was soon up to full speed and made its usual good progress through the industrial cities that line the southern end of Lake Michigan. But, after we headed northwest and crossed the border into Michigan, we encountered the first of the problems that was to plague the balance of our trip. A hard freezing rain blanketed the landscape. Apparently it had been coming down most of the day and all the limbs on the hundreds of trees that lined the railroad right of way were laden with heavy ice. Our forward progress slowed dramatically and eventually the train ground to a halt. We peered out the windows and wondered what the problem was. The conductor answered our query by describing the ice-covered limbs that had fallen across the tracks ahead. He said the engineer was waiting for a railroad crew to saw them into manageable sizes and remove them from the right of way. The train remained there for about twenty minutes and then slowly continued on its way. Perhaps half an hour later the same thing happened again. The balance of the ride was a study in frustration as there were ice-covered limbs down all long the entire route. Our train covered the final one hundred and seventy-five miles to our destination at Flint in record breaking time. <u>Record breaking for slowness, that is!</u> Normally it takes about six hours to travel the route from Chicago to Flint. That night it took more than ten hours.

About 2:00 the next morning, we inched our way into the city and came to a halt beside the station at Flint. At that point we assumed our trials and tribulations for the trip were over. Not so! After grabbing our luggage we headed in the direction of the lot where our car had been parked since the previous Friday afternoon.

There we found the nearly unrecognizable car looking like a giant irregularly shaped ice cube! More than a half inch of ice covered every surface. Because we were unable to open either the car doors or the trunk; we couldn't get to the ice scrapers there. So each of us took a house key and began to scrape laboriously at the ice on the doors. Finally, after half an hour of very intensive toil, we were able to use the key to get inside. Then the job of clearing the accumulated ice from the windshield and rear window went faster because we could use the scrapers and the car's heater was in operation.

The sixty mile route from Flint to our home in Midland was ice-covered and treacherous. We could average no more than twenty miles per hour the entire way. It was after 6:00 a.m. before we reached the relative comfort and safety of home—utterly exhausted from the ordeal. Our exhilarating weekend trek to the Windy City had at last come to a stress-filled and disappointing end.

A 1995 summer rail trip to Chicago is even more difficult for me to forget. Once again a friend and I booked reservations on the westbound Amtrack train to Chicago from Flint. We drove there, boarded the passenger car and shortly were on our way westward. By the time we cleared the city limits the train was nearly at full speed. Many rural villages like Swartz Creek, Lennon, Durand, Laingsburg and De Witt border Flint to the west and form satellite communities there. Passing through those satellite towns the train tracks intersect with a large number of roads and highways as they make their way along the right of way. Some of the intersections have overpasses, others use crossing gates and a few merely have flashing cautionary lights to warn the drivers of an approaching locomotive.

That afternoon we were seated in the passenger car immediately behind the engine. My seat was next to the window on the right facing the front of the train. As we traveled along I looked out the window at the passing parade of small towns and rural Michigan scenery. It was summer and the state was having one of its rare pleasantly warm and sunny days. Summer days in Michigan often are hot and uncomfortably sultry. The weather and visibility were perfect that day.

While looking out the window I noticed that we were approaching the intersection of a country road near the town of Swartz Creek. A short distance to the south a black pickup truck sped along the road toward the train tracks. My angle of vision made it impossible for

45

me to see the intersection ahead where the tracks met the road. I
just assumed that there must be an overpass there and the pickup
would pass under the train on its way along the road.

That was a totally incorrect assumption. The pickup disappeared
from my view just as I heard a loud "thump" and felt the train jolt
and shudder violently before continuing on its way. "My God" I
thought, "Was the pickup actually hit by the train?" My question
was answered when the engineer immediately began to apply
the brakes. Because the train had been traveling at a fast clip, it
continued more than a mile before finally coming to a grinding halt
on the tracks next to a farmer's cornfield.

Once the locomotive stopped we looked at one another in
puzzlement. Momentarily the conductor came by and related that
there had been an accident and asked us to remain on the train. I
told my traveling companion what I had seen and soon the entire car
was buzzing with wild conjecture about the incident and its possible
aftermath. We were forced to wait for a time before we learned
anything more about what had occurred.

Eventually a railroad official appeared to tell us that he and
others were conducting an investigation of the accident and wanted
our full cooperation. He asked if anyone had seen the vehicle before
it was struck by the train. I told him that I had seen it traveling on
the road. He took my name and left the car. In a few minutes he
returned with another official and they interviewed me in minute
detail.

They questioned me concerning exactly where I was sitting, toward what direction I was looking, and if I had been able to see the crossing lights at the intersection. They particularly wanted to know if the lights were flashing at the time of the incident. I'm afraid that I was of little help. Even though I did see the pickup as it approached the intersection, I wasn't able to see the crossing lights from my angle of vision. I mentioned that it had been my incorrect assumption there must be an overpass at the junction. After asking innumerable questions they took down my address and telephone number before going on to question other witnesses to the accident.

The investigation continued for several hours before the train was able to move along on its interrupted way to Chicago. Much later we learned that the pickup was being driven by a teen-aged boy out joy-riding with his even younger girlfriend. Apparently he totally ignored the flashing cautionary lights as he attempted to outrun the train at the intersection. The boy lost the race and thus was struck by the locomotive. That race turned out to be his final one because he and the girl died instantly in the melee. The youngster had needlessly sacrificed his own life and, more tragically, had sacrificed the life of his young companion as well. Debris from the pickup was scattered along the entire way from the point of impact to where the train finally came to a halt a mile down the tracks.

When finally it arrived at Chicago's Union Station; the train was over three hours behind schedule. Though badly shaken by the tragedy, we were still curious enough to sneak a quick look

47

at the front of the locomotive to see the destruction caused by the impact. The damage was severe and bits of the black pickup still clung to the engine's wrinkled surface. My own quick look at the result convinced me that I would never attempt to outrun a train at an intersection.

Originally we had booked the trip to Chicago for pure enjoyment but that was difficult to do after witnessing such a deplorable event. The accident cast a pall over us that lasted well after we returned home to Michigan. My memory of the "clunk" made by the black pickup and the locomotive as they collided is as vivid now as it was the day it occurred.

From those two incidents on Chicago train rides, I learned that a normally dull and prosaic action could end up being far from dull and prosaic. However, none of the trials and tribulations encountered along the way ever discourage me from train travel. I still ride the rails as often as opportunities present themselves.

# CHAPTER 5
# THE SENIOR TRIP AND BEYOND

Near the end of June in 1949, the year I was graduated from Vassar High School, the mailman stopped in front of our farm and left the day's accumulation of mail. As always I was curious to see what he had brought so I hurried out to the mailbox. To my amazement when I retrieved the mail; there, smiling up at me from the cover of Life Magazine, was a familiar face—someone whom I knew personally. To the best of my recollection that is the one and only time a photograph of an acquaintance of mine has ever been on the cover of a national magazine.

The girl's name was Marsha Mattson and she too was a member of the 1949 high school graduation class. However, she lived in Hillsdale, a small town near the Michigan/Ohio border. I had met

Marsha a couple of months previous to that day in the engine room of the S.S. Noronic, a cruise ship that plied the waters of the Great Lakes. Yes, I did say <u>in the engine room</u>!

To explain how that happened let me digress a bit. For their senior trips that year the graduating classes of both Vassar and Hillsdale chose to go on a five day cruise through Lake Erie and Lake Ontario. The seniors from both schools worked hard all year sponsoring money-making events to help defray the cost of the cruise. Finally the day in May arrived and we were on our way to meet the ship in Detroit.

With much fanfare we boarded the majestic ship, the S. S. Noronic, at the port in Detroit and sailed down the Detroit River. I recall vividly that the song "Cruising down the River" was popular at the time and we nearly wore out our lungs and the patience of anyone listening while we sang its lyrics over and over again. The Detroit River empties into Lake Erie some twenty-five miles or so south of the city. From there we sailed east across the length of Lake Erie in order to make a stopover at Buffalo, New York. At Buffalo we were able to disembark and explore the city. The incident I recall best about our departure from Buffalo was that several of my classmates became falling-down drunk and nearly missed the ship's sailing. During the next twenty-four hours, while they recovered from their hangovers, those individuals hardly appeared on deck at all.

Once we had everyone aboard the ship again, we by-passed Niagara Falls and traveled from Lake Erie to Lake Ontario through the Welland Canal. The canal has eight locks along its twenty-seven mile course. The locks lower ships 326 feet below Lake Erie and down to the level of Lake Ontario. I was captivated watching the ship carefully maneuvering into the locks with mere inches to spare. When the gigantic gates were closed the ship descended ever so slowly as the water level fell.

Along the canal's route we sailed past the picturesque Canadian cities of Port Colbourne, Welland, Thorold, St. Catharines and lastly Port Weller at the north end. Passage through the locks took most of a day before we entered Lake Ontario. Then we sailed the short distance across the western end of Lake Ontario to Toronto, Canada. The cruise ship docked at Toronto and spent most of the day in port while we had time to tour the city and take in its sightseeing possibilities. That was the last port of call before we began the return trip. The cruise ended back at Detroit where it had begun five days earlier.

Now let's go back to the question, "How did I meet Marsha Mattson in the ship's engine room?" Shortly after we boarded at Detroit and were well underway, the ship's crew began conducting guided tours throughout the vessel. I found the engine room to be the most fascinating part of the tour. It was a huge enclosure probably fifty feet from end to end which was kept in spotlessly clean condition. On that first visit I stood next to the twenty foot horizontal connecting rods that moved the giant pistons in and out of the cylinders and was absolutely in awe of their massive power; plus I was amazed at how smoothly they moved to and fro. The friendly engineers on duty there explained the technicalities of how a steamship is propelled. They added that we were welcome to come to the engine room at other times while on the cruise if we wished to do so. That was all the invitation I needed.

During the next five days I spent much time in the engine room. In fact, there was a small clique of us (perhaps five) that regularly met there to talk with the crewmen and observe the mesmerizing mechanism in operation. Marsha Mattson was one of the members of that group. She appeared to be equally as fascinated as I with the place and the massive steam engine. While our classmates partied or sunned themselves on the decks above, our little circle spent many hours in the areas below. The crewmen came to know us and apparently enjoyed our appreciation of their roles in running the vast ship. The various members of our select little group came to know one another well and thoroughly enjoyed the get-togethers in our "private domain." Marsha was my favorite from the clique. She was a beautiful and intelligent young lady with a marvelous sense of humor and, in addition, possessed a warm and winning personality. We became good friends over the next few days. Before the cruise was over, I had a typical teenager's "crush" on her.

But let's go back to the beginning of my little tale. Why was Marsha's picture on the cover of Life Magazine a short two months later? Hurriedly I flipped through the magazine until I reached page 82 where the story began. After scanning the article, I learned that the 1949 Hillsdale High School graduation class had been chosen by the editors of the magazine to be featured in that June issue. Besides Marsha's photograph on the cover, there was a ten-page spread on the inside with pictures and stories about some of her one hundred and one fellow classmates. The article contained snippets of information about the most popular girl, the valedictorian, the class artist, the class clown, the drum majorette, the newspaper editor, the class president and even described one student who ran away from home because he feared he would flunk out and not graduate with the class. It is my belief that the editors of <u>Life Magazine</u> agreed with me that Marsha was both attractive and photogenic. Therefore, from all the members of the graduating class, they chose her to adorn the cover of the popular national magazine. She was the perfect choice in my estimation.

Nearly a year later I met and became well acquainted with one of Marsha's fellow classmates—a young man named David Hayhow. In the <u>Life Magazine</u> article, David was featured prominently with both a photo and a story because he was the editor of Hillsdale's school newspaper. The piece explained that he was the son of the local newspaper editor and that he would be majoring in journalism at Michigan State that fall. The photo showed David writing his final editorial for the school paper. The article about him ended with this quote, "This time, as always, he has let the chore go until the very last minute." Considering later developments in our lives, I think that was a most prophetic statement.

Michigan State was where I met David but that didn't happen until the beginning of the third term of my freshman year there. My brother, Laurel, and I both enrolled at State in the fall of 1949. I was assigned a room on the second floor of Mason Hall with two other freshmen from Marshall, Michigan. Temporarily, Laurel was assigned a cubicle in a Quonset Hut on the South Campus. Near the Quonset Huts south of the river, two new residential dormitories, West Shaw Hall and East Shaw Hall, were under construction. When West Shaw was completed at Christmas time, Laurel moved there.

East Shaw Hall was slated for completion in February, 1950. Laurel and I wanted to room together so we asked to be assigned to a three-man room there for the final term which would began in April. At the time we had no idea who our other roommate would be. When the time came the two of us moved our things into the second floor corner room and soon were greeted by the third occupant. It was David Hayhow from Hillsdale.

Roommates come in a variety of sizes, shapes, colors and attitudes. I remember writing a college essay on that subject for my sophomore English literature class. My little exposé described some roommates as being considerate, friendly, helpful, cooperative and fun to live with. Other roommates, I wrote, were selfish, mean, inconsiderate, manipulative, and nearly impossible to live with.

David fell somewhere between the two extremes. At times he was friendly and other times he was aloof and moody. Upon occasion he was cooperative about keeping the room neat and clean but, at other times he left his area and ours in total shambles. "I'll do it later!" was his usual response when confronted. Originally Laurel and I intended to do much of our studying in the dormitory room but David either did no studying at all or did it elsewhere. He was very popular and, with his many friends, was noisy enough that studying in the dormitory proved impossible.

Laurel and I generally agreed on the vast majority of issues. David learned early on that if we brothers were in accord on any subject he would get nowhere in opposing us. Later he employed the age-old war tactic of "divide and conquer" by campaigning for his hair-brained schemes with us separately. Sometimes the plan worked, but usually he met with utter defeat.

David used his fertile imagination for dreaming up many zany ideas. One evening when we came back to the room and switched on the overhead light, the entire room was bathed in a kaleidoscope of colors. While we were gone he had taken the glass globe down from the ceiling fixture and carefully glued small pieces of colored tissue paper over its entire surface before replacing it. The effect was interesting but the diffused light couldn't illuminate all parts of the room and having paper against the hot surface posed a fire danger as well. We told David that the tissue paper had to come down. David refused. Taking matters into my own hands, I removed the paper and replaced the globe. He was furious, but knew that he was seriously outnumbered on the issue. The globe remained free of tissue paper.

By the end of the three month spring term Laurel and I had our fill with David and his antics. We were more than ready to bid our roommate a not so fond goodbye for the summer. Ironically neither Laurel nor I returned to Michigan State the next fall. Laurel began a course at General Motors Technical Institute and I stayed out of college for a year in order to earn the necessary money to return the following year.

Fifty-plus years have elapsed since I last saw either Marsha Mattson or David Hayhow. During that half century I have seldom even thought of the two, however, several years ago, while looking through an antique shop in Saginaw, Michigan, I was reminded of them once again.

One of the antique vendors in the store had a collection of old Life Magazines. Out of curiosity I began thumbing through them and suddenly I remembered the issue that featured the Hillsdale graduating class. Quickly I dropped the magazine I was holding and searched for the one with Marsha's photograph on its cover. It wasn't in the collection! I asked the vendor if he knew of anywhere I could obtain that issue of Life. He indicated there should be no problem in locating one. The vendor pointed me in the direction of several other antique shops in town that usually carried old magazines.

Finally, several weeks later I located the copy that I have today. The price I paid for that one issue was written on the plastic covering--$4.25. On the cover of the magazine proper, under Marsha's photo, was the 1949 price for a yearly subscription of 52 issues. That price was $6.00!

# CHAPTER 6
# FAMILIAR FACES IN STRANGE PLACES ·

The bartender in a downtown pub on Chicago's Michigan Avenue smiled as he handed me my drink and asked, "Do you know who is sitting next to you?" I was spending a December weekend in the Windy City and had just come in from the frigid, blustery street to take the first seat I saw. It was on the end of a horseshoe-shaped bar. After ordering the drink from the bartender, I shrugged out of my winter jacket and hung it on a rack in the corner. Up to that point I hadn't particularly noticed other patrons in the establishment. However, the bartender's question piqued my curiosity so I turned to the gentleman beside me and studied him carefully. The graying, red-haired bar patron sitting there; who likely was in his early sixties, smiled at me in return. His face did look somewhat familiar, but for the moment his name wouldn't come to mind. At that point I had no clue as to who the man was.

The stranger and I exchanged small talk for a few moments while I pondered his identity. Then, as I listened to the distinctive voice and took note of the lopsided grin, suddenly I recognized him! He was the well-known dancer and singer, Dan Dailey, of Broadway, movie and television fame. I remembered him most recently from the popular television series "The Governor and J.J." with Julie Sommars. The tall, red-haired singer and dancer, who co-starred in many post World War II movies with the likes of Betty Grable, Ethel Merman, Jeanie Crain and Jayne Mansfield, always impressed me with his fantastic dancing ability. Back then he was a renowned "hoofer" and was even nominated for an academy award in 1948.

Once the mystery was solved, I introduced myself and the two of us shook hands. Mr. Dailey seemed pleased that I finally did recognize him. Though he still was a handsome man, he had changed much in appearance from when he was in his prime. He had gained some weight, and now had prominent jowls on either side of his once long, narrow face. Most of his still abundant hair was gray, but I could make out vestiges of its former carrot red color. Mr. Dailey was dressed casually in a pair of dark slacks, a light colored long-sleeved shirt and a burgundy sports coat. I'm at a loss to remember what kind of drink he was nursing.

While sipping our drinks; we chatted back and forth. During that conversation I confessed to him that at one time I entertained aspirations of being an actor but instead had settled for doing amateur acting in local productions. I told him that I was a secondary school teacher. His reply indicated that he thought both of our career choices were difficult undertakings. In answer to my next question of why he was in Chicago, Mr. Dailey told me that he was starring in the comedy "The Odd Couple" which was having a short run at one of the city's theatres. He was playing one of the two leads in the cast for the touring Broadway show.

I found the famous actor to be a real gentleman as he answered my many questions. He even asked me a few questions as well. Mr. Dailey appeared to have a genuine interest in what I had to say and carefully listened to my answers. Later, when I was ready to leave the pub and head out into the cold again on the way to my hotel, I shook his hand for the second time and told him that it had been a real pleasure meeting him and hoped that it would happen again.

Unfortunately that second meeting never occurred. About a year after that, in 1975, I read in the *Detroit Free Press,* that Mr. Dailey had passed away suddenly. His death ended a long, busy career in show business spanning well over forty years—from when he was a teenager until he was in his mid-sixties. To him I say, "Rest well, Mr. Dailey. You earned it."

Another time that I encountered a familiar face in a strange place was in Rome during the summer of 1966. For several weeks I had been traveling around Western Europe visiting different cities on my itinerary. By the time I arrived in Rome I had already visited Copenhagen, Denmark; Oslo, Norway; both East and West Berlin and Frankfurt, West Germany. My last stop on the mainland of Europe was to be in the Eternal City.

Well before the trip began my American travel bureau made all of the airplane and room reservations in advance. So after I arrived at the airport, I took a shuttle bus to the downtown hotel, registered and unpacked my suitcases. After consulting a city map I discovered that the Roman Forum was within easy walking distance from where I was staying. The entire afternoon lay ahead of me so I decided to go exploring at the historic site.

There were guided tours of the area every hour on the hour and I purchased a ticket for an English-speaking tour. Unlike most American tourist attractions, many of those in other areas of the world cater to English-speaking travelers by conducting tours in their own language. That is a distinct convenience for the thousands of Americans who travel abroad each year and have no foreign language ability. Officials of American tourist attractions could learn much from Europeans in that regard.

In prehistoric times there was a swamp where the Roman Forum lies today between three of the famous Seven Hills of Rome—the Palatine, the Capitoline and the Viminal. That early swamp was drained and its area was transformed into a market place. Later it became the governmental center for both the Roman Republic and the Roman Empire. After the empire was overtaken by the Barbarians the Forum fell into disuse and much of it was covered by soil and debris. Since the early 1800's the Italian government has excavated the buildings that remain and thousands of tourists from all over the world visit the Forum daily.

After obtaining my admission ticket, I went down a stairway to the ancient street level which was about 20 feet lower than the modern street above. There I joined the other members of the tour and met the tour guide. While we walked through the ancient streets the guide explained the former purposes of such buildings as the *Curia*, or Senate House, the triumphal arch of Septimus Severus, the temple of Saturn and the Basilica of Julia. He also pointed out the only wide street that crosses the Forum, the *Via Sacra*, or sacred street. It was along that ancient way that the Roman Emperors and generals paraded their captives and other spoils of war after returning from victorious foreign campaigns around the Mediterranean Sea.

Ancient history has always been one of my avid interests and I was thrilled to be walking in the exact same places where figures like Julius Caesar, Nero, Marcus Aurelius and Augustus had once walked. I paid very little attention to my tour companions as we slowly made our way across the Forum. After all, I had come to the Eternal City to see and experience what it had to offer, not to waste my time hobnobbing with other tourists.

Suddenly a male voice from the tour group startled me by saying, "Pardon me, but aren't you Jerry Davis from Saginaw, Michigan?"

After quickly turning toward the speaker in surprise, but not immediately knowing who he was, I stammered, "Yes, I am." "I thought so." replied the man, "I'm Bill Olsen, also from Saginaw." Apparently I didn't recognize him because of not expecting to see anyone from home on a walking tour in Rome. Once I regained my composure, I greeted him in a more friendly way and we shook hands. Bill and I were not close friends at home but we had met one another on several occasions at parties and had many mutual friends as well.

I must confess that neither of us learned anything more about the Roman Forum from the tour beyond that point. Bill was as curious as I about what had brought the two of us to the exact same place at the same time over three thousand miles from Saginaw. I explained that I was on a three-week excursion visiting some of the major cities in Europe and that Rome happened to be my next to the last stop before returning to the United States. Bill told me that his employer, Dow Chemical Corporation which has its headquarters in Midland, Michigan, had sent him to Rome on company business. During his only free afternoon and evening, Bill decided to see a few of the sightseeing possibilities before he left the city. He was scheduled to fly out the next day.

We made arrangements to meet at my hotel later that afternoon. After going out for dinner together and gorging ourselves on wonderful Italian cuisine, we worked off some of the extra poundage by walking to the Coliseum. We calculated the distance was a little over three miles from the restaurant and both agreed that seeing the ruin was well worth the hike. Bill left the next day and I continued on my tour.

I encountered yet another familiar face in a strange place during one of my spring vacations while I was teaching at a junior high school after moving to Midland, Michigan. During that ten day break from school, another teacher and I made arrangements to go on a driving trip to Kentucky. We visited several different points of interest during the trip. The first of those was Senator Henry Clay's estate, called Ashland, on the outskirts of Lexington. Clay was particularly well-known for his many attempts to hold the Union together prior to the Civil War. In addition, he ran for president three times but was defeated each time.

A few miles south of Lexington we toured a strange religious colony at Shakertown. The Shakers made up a small religious sect that had its start in England. Their name derived from claims of receiving a religious power causing them to shake and tremble. They held regular worship sessions where the men did a sort of dance on one side of the hall and the women did the same on the other side. Shakers did not believe in marriage or having children so all increases to their group had to come through converts to their faith.

Moving on to Bardstown we visited the Rowan residence which is called "My Old Kentucky Home". The Rowan's cousin, Stephen Foster, is reputed to have written his well-known song by that name while visiting the family at the house. Whether or not the story is true, the present owners are deriving a good income by conducting guided tours through the residence.

Our final visit in Kentucky before returning to Michigan was at Mammoth Cave National Park. It was early afternoon when we arrived there and, after checking into the park's motel, went exploring. Our tour of the caves was scheduled for the next morning so we had a few hours to satisfy our curiosity about the park. We wandered for several hours through the grounds paying little heed to where we stepped. Later in our motel room we saw a sign stating, "NOTICE! DO NOT STRAY FROM THE PAVED PATHS IN THE PARK! NUMEROUS RATTLESNAKES INHABIT THE AREA!" In that case ignorance was bliss because we saw no reptiles of any kind.

While on our little walk we checked out the natural historic entrance to the caves. At that time there were three routes into the 150 mile labyrinth: (1) the natural entrance, (2) a steep stairway built into the ledge rock atop the caves and (3) by elevator. We had read that the natural entrance was blocked off a couple of hundred feet inside, but our curiosity made us want to see what it looked like anyway. It turned out to be a rough hole in the side of a stone hill. The surprising fact about it was that it was large enough to drive a locomotive through without touching the sides or the top. We followed a paved path into the cave and walked until we were stopped by a locked gate. Other tourists were curious about seeing the historic entrance too, because there we found a vacationing family of four exploring the formations as well.

Immediately upon our arrival we heard one of the children in the family say to another, "Isn't that Mr. Baldwin and Mr. Davis?" That comment caught our attention and we looked at the group more carefully. We knew them! They were Mr. and Mrs. Cal Miller and their two children—in effect, neighbors of ours. Cal was a high school principal in the same system where my friend and I taught! Like us, the Miller family had taken advantage of the school's spring break to visit Mammoth Caves. The six of us enthused about how eerie it was that we should happen to meet nearly five hundred miles from home with no prior knowledge of one another's travel plans.

Mexico City was the setting for another meeting with a familiar face in a strange place. In 1986, shortly before I retired from teaching in Midland, that same teacher friend and I spent Easter and the week following in the Mexican capital. Our hotel, the Prim, was a couple of blocks off *Paseo de la Reforma*, the main thoroughfare bisecting the city center. That central location allowed us to walk to many of the points of interest. For example, the *Zona Rosa* or Pink Zone, an enclave with restaurants, shops and entertainment, was nearby, as were open air markets, museums, and many historic sites. The governmental center called the *Zocalo* and the Palace of Fine Arts where the *Ballet Folklorico* was performed were less than a half hour by foot. Consequently, we did a great deal of walking over the next ten days. The tourist attractions in more remote areas—not within walking distance—could be reached using the subway system.

During our first few days in Mexico City we became familiar with the huge metropolis and even developed favorites among the many restaurants that dotted the downtown area. Two of them were real standouts. In the *Zona Rosa* there was a steak house that served mouthwatering steaks for very reasonable prices. We went there night after night and, while we enjoyed our steaks, musicians wandered about the restaurant entertaining the patrons.

The other restaurant which became special to us was Shirley's on the Paseo de la Reforma. It was only a few short blocks from our hotel and we went there often for breakfast or lunch. One afternoon, after a day of sightseeing, we returned to the hotel to stash our souvenirs and other purchases. We decided that we were hungry and one of us suggested a walk over to Shirley's for an early dinner. The weather was sunny and warm. It was just the right sort of day for a short walk particularly when the prospect of a good meal awaited us at its end.

When we arrived at the front of the restaurant and were about to enter, my friend noticed a woman who was just exiting the establishment. He turned to me and said, "That lady looks just like Bev Orr!" He felt confident enough about her identity to approach her and ask. Yes, she was Bev! She was equally surprised to see him as he was to see her. Bev and my friend had both grown up in Midland. In fact he dated her sister for a short time. They only saw one another rarely after Bev left Midland for college and later began her career. We learned that she was teaching school on the western side of Michigan in the Grand Rapids area. Like the two of us, she was off for the spring break and also like us, had opted to spend some of her free time in Mexico City. We decided that it was a strange occurrence, indeed, when we could come across someone from our home town in a location over two thousand miles distant.

Probably there are many additional examples of meeting familiar faces in strange places that I could have described in this vignette. The four examples mentioned above, however, serve to illustrate that coming into contact with people you know doesn't only occur near home. It can and does happen in distant locations as well. When claiming that the world is getting smaller, one is stating an obvious truism.

# CHAPTER 7
# TRAVELING SOUTH OF THE BORDER

"Welcome to Puerto Vallarta. Please remain in your seats with your seatbelts fastened. We are sorry to announce that there will be a slight delay before any passengers may leave for the terminal. The pilot was forced to land the aircraft on a flat tire." With that the flight attendant put down the microphone with a noisy clack. WHAT DID SHE SAY? LANDED ON A FLAT TIRE? Little wonder that our airplane had made a rather uncharacteristically rough landing at the resort city's airport. A friend and I were on the next to the last leg of a Mexicana Airlines flight from Detroit, Michigan and our final destination was Mexico City.

That was our first time experiencing a flat tire on an aircraft. We were a bit shocked and even more curious about what would happen next. As we watched out the windows, a crowd of approximately twenty Mexican men appeared at the side of the airplane. Two of them had brought tools along and they began removing the culprit wheel with the flat tire. The rest of the men carefully watched every part of the procedure. I wasn't certain what their purpose was in being there. Was it to learn how to change a tire on an airplane or to see that the two who were actually doing the work, did it properly? Regardless of that question which had no available answer, the tire eventually was replaced. Soon the crowd dispersed and the aircraft continued across the tarmac.

Rather than rolling all the way to the terminal however, it stopped short of it at a long, narrow one-story building. Once again the flight attendant came on the loudspeaker to make an announcement. "Because of the extra long stop here at Puerto Vallarta, all passengers, whether remaining here or flying on, will be required to go through a customs check. Please exit the aircraft, pick up your luggage, and proceed to the Customs Hall." We located our bags, were herded into the stifling one-story building and formed ourselves into lines in front of the officials according to the initials of our last names.

The two of us happened to be near the front of our line so the official was finished with us in a relatively short time. Because the building had no air conditioning, it was uncomfortably hot. All the windows and doors were closed and there was no air movement of any kind. My friend and I noticed a door at the far end of the room and walked to it. After opening the door, we stepped out and stood just outside under an overhang enjoying the vestige of a breeze that we found there.

In a flash one of the customs men bustled outside and officiously directed us to remain inside the building until the other passengers had finished and then all would re-board the airplane. Apparently we formed some sort of security risk when not pent up in the unbearably hot and sticky Customs Hall. Grudgingly we returned to the tropical interior and waited for our fellow passengers to finish. Finally the customs check was completed and we were once again airborne and on our way to Mexico City. I have been to Mexico four times but that was my only visit to the popular resort city of Puerto Vallarta and, though brief, it left a decidedly unpleasant taste in my mouth.

After saying that however, I must confess that Mexico remains one of my favorite travel destinations. The country has seemingly unlimited sightseeing possibilities, the people are friendly, and the country has to be counted among the least expensive places I have ever visited. Numerous devaluations of the Mexican peso against the dollar have served to make most prices well within anyone's reach. For example, the last time I spent a few days in Mexico City, I paid only $9.00 a night for a room with a private bath at a nice hotel only three blocks off the main street, *Paseo de la Reforma*, and only a short walk from the city center. Even the least expensive room at any Motel-6 in America tends to be a minimum of three times that costly.

Inherently, travel in any foreign country may provide the setting for minor confrontations or sticky situations merely because two different societies come face to face with one another. What is accepted and common practice in one country often is considered bad taste in another. While reminiscing about travel in Mexico several interesting and possibly amusing incidents come to mind. The following are a few good examples.

On my second trip to Mexico City, probably in 1987, my traveling companion and I set out to absorb some of the local color and activities by walking through the neighborhoods that were not part of the usual tourist haunts. Perhaps ten blocks south of our hotel we came upon an impressive market with many different vendors selling everything from sides of beef and fresh fish to garden produce and various fruits.

The market was simply crawling with people buying groceries or merely chatting with acquaintances in the crowded aisles. As we approached the entrance to the emporium we were greeted with the usual number of beggars that frequent all public places in Mexico. Because we stood out as obvious foreigners, we were immediately accosted. Our normal reaction to beggars was to give them a few pesos and continue on our way. Most beggars were poorly clothed, undernourished and appeared to be truly needy. However, the two men who asked us for a handout were hardly the usual type. They were decently-dressed, clean and appeared healthy and well-fed. Our first thought was that they were part of a very profitable scam. Therefore we pretended not to understand their pleas for money and entered the market without contributing. As we passed I heard one mutter loudly, "Los americanos estupidos! (Stupid Americans!)." Perhaps we were stupid Americans but we were not stupid enough to be taken in by their transparently false neediness.

We spent a half hour or so wandering around the market enjoying the ambience, the noisy haggling and even the pungent aromas of the meats and the produce being traded in the establishment. Swarms of flies appeared to be enjoying the business place equally as much as we were. After exiting the emporium, we came upon yet another curious but interesting bit of Mexicana. Parking in all of Mexico City is at a premium. The city, often estimated at over twenty million inhabitants, appears to have an equal number of cars. Sometimes they are parked four abreast along the major streets. That is two beside one another on the street itself and two on the sidewalk next to the street.

As we worked our way around the illegally parked cars on the sidewalk we saw a young girl with someone likely her little brother. The boy, only four or five years old, was urinating on the tire of one of the parked cars. The young girl, probably several years older and obviously in charge of her little brother, was helpfully holding the boy's penis so that he wouldn't wet his clothing. I felt that in the little girl's case, she <u>was</u> her brother's keeper. And, she was doing a commendable job of it.

Our hotel of choice each time we have visited Mexico City, is the comparatively small Hotel Prim. In its first floor lobby is a travel or sightseeing desk. There we could sign up for various mini-bus tours to some of the attractions in and around the huge metropolis. Previously, we had visited the Pyramids of Teotihuacan, the Ballet Folklorico, and the Zocalo using the travel desk. One day I noticed a sign there announcing a bus trip to the city of Tula.

Tula is famous for its palace ruins and, more particularly, for its huge monolithic statues of gods. Many of the statues are over twenty feet tall. I had read much about the site and wanted to go there. We signed up for the trip and early the next morning met the bus driver at the designated location outside the hotel entrance. The bus driver started off on the wrong foot by showing up more than a half hour late in meeting us. Once we were inside the mini-bus and on the way to pick up other passengers, he compounded the problem by casually announcing that since too few people had signed up for the Tula trip, he was combining two groups and we would be going to the city of Toluca instead. That too didn't set well with either of us as we wanted to see Tula, not Toluca.

The next half hour was spent gathering additional passengers until the mini-bus was more than crowded. It was packed! We were both fuming with frustration. Fortunately, we had not had to pay a deposit for our trip reservation, so I whispered to my friend, "At the next stop light we are going to get out of the bus." We happened to be sitting in the front seats next to the door. When the bus came to a halt, I announced that we were leaving the tour. The driver said, "You can't do that." I replied, "Yes we can." My friend opened the door and we stepped out on to the sidewalk. The light changed to green and we waved goodbye as the driver was forced to move ahead in the flow of the traffic.

With an entire empty day yawning before us, we decided to visit the Zona Rosa, a popular entertainment, dining and shopping area. We boarded a subway car and soon were on our way across the city. After arriving, while crossing one of the Zona's busy streets, we discussed our disappointment about not seeing Tula. We were overheard by a young man walking near us. He asked, "Would you like to go to Tula? I am a taxi driver and would be happy to take you there." We asked what he would charge for the day-long trip. It was less than the bus trip to Toluca! So we immediately agreed to his proposition.

The driver, whose name was Ramon, showed us to his taxi which was parked nearby and we started on what was likely the best of the mini-tours we ever took while in Mexico. Not only did Ramon drive us to the ruins and giant statuary at Tula, but he read all the Spanish signs at the sites and translated them into English for us. He was a knowledgeable and entertaining companion to us for the rest of the day. We told him the sad tale of our aborted bus trip and how we had ended up in the Zona Rosa where we met him.

The three of us agreed that it was a most fortuitous meeting for all concerned.

Our first trip to Mexico City was a couple of years prior to the great Michoacan Earthquake of September 19, 1985. The quake, which measured 8.1 on the Richter Scale, had its epicenter a few miles southwest of the city and, in all, took the lives of more than 9,000 people. In Mexico City the loss of life was enormous because the tremors caused a large number of tall buildings to collapse, crushing everyone inside. Only a very few of those trapped individuals were ever pulled to safety.

Back in Michigan we read about the earthquake and saw its disastrous results on television and wondered if our friend, Joaquin Palacios, who lived in an apartment at the former Olympic Village and taught at the University of Mexico City, had survived the tragedy. After a number of failed attempts to telephone him, we heard about a ham radio operator in Michigan who was in contact with other operators in the beleaguered city. Finally after about a week had elapsed we learned that he and his apartment building had both survived.

When we made reservations at the travel bureau for our next trip to Mexico, we received the good news that the Hotel Prim, where we had stayed previously, still stood in spite of the earthquake. During that second trip we had some very somber moments as we walked past a number of the large buildings that had been reduced to what looked like a large plate of pancakes. The vertical walls had disappeared and all that remained were cement floors stacked one upon another. Fortunately, most of the beautiful old historic buildings such as the Federal Government Building, called the *Zocalo*, the Palace of Fine Arts, the Castle of Chapultepec, the ancient Basilica of Guadalupe and the National Cathedral, all survived the earthquake. Ironically, the older buildings could withstand the tremors, while it was the newer, modern buildings that were unable to do so.

On a somewhat lighter note, arriving and departing by air from Mexico City can be an adventure. The airport, which probably was more than adequate when it was built, now is a tight squeeze for the newer and larger super aircraft like the Boeing 747's that regularly fly in and out. Expansion is impossible because the facility is hemmed in on three sides by the city itself and on the other by the encroaching mountains such as the ever snow-capped Iztaccihuatl and its nearby twin Popocatepetl. Consequently, landings and take offs from Mexico City must be done at a sharper angle than is considered safe at most other large international airports. When one is approaching from the air, the landing area appears to be postage stamp-sized and far too small to accommodate large airplanes. Rumor has it that only well-seasoned pilots land and take off from that facility. I'm very pleased to report that all of my arrivals or departures from the city have been uneventful. Apparently experienced pilots were at the controls.

The first time I flew into the Mexico City Airport, our plane remained out on the tarmac at a good distance from the terminal. I wondered why and soon my curiosity was satisfied when a large bus lumbered toward us. As it neared the airplane, the body of the bus rose on scissor-like legs. That brought it on a level with the airplane exit door and we were able to walk directly from the plane's cabin into the waiting bus. On the drive to the terminal building the legs scissored downward once again. Then we exited from the bus into the terminal at the lower level.

I would be remiss if I ended the story of our travels in Mexico, without mentioning the "Great Jelly Bean Caper". A short time prior to leaving Mexico City on our second trip, my traveling companion purchased a paper sack of the small-sized jelly beans, called Jelly Bellys. When we were packing our luggage at the hotel, he put them in his carry-on bag for the trip home. We boarded the bus for the ride to the airport and neither of us thought any more about the candy resting in the bag.

At the airport security checkpoint my friend placed the carry-on bag atop the conveyor belt and it proceeded into the x-ray machine. The attendant eyed the image on the x-ray screen suspiciously and when the carry-on came out the other end, he picked it up and asked my friend to open it for him. The man began rummaging in the interior and pulled out the sack of jelly beans. Later we decided that on the x-ray screen they must have resembled drug capsules and thus they aroused his suspicions. When he pulled the paper sack from the bag, the sack tore and jelly beans scattered across the surface of the moving conveyor belt. Immediately the attendant saw his mistake and flushed crimson. Guiltily, he attempted to scoop up some of the bouncing jelly beans and put them back into the torn sack. My friend objected, not wanting the soiled candy in with the clean. The whole scene became a riot of confusion as the two struggled with the jelly bean sack. I noticed other waiting passengers laughing gleefully. Finally the attendant gave up and motioned my friend to go on through without the spilled jelly beans. The obvious moral of this story is: "Do not attempt to smuggle Jelly Bellys out of Mexico City because the officials will catch you every time!"

For any traveler like me who is interested in ancient history, Mexico is of particular interest. The capital city has enormous ruins which pre-date the Spanish Conquest era and are from the days of the Aztecs. In one of the underground subway stations there is a ruin that was discovered when the station was excavated. The excavators left the ruin and built the station around it. It is still on view today. A few miles from the city, the ancient Teotihuacanos built the Pyramid of the Sun and the Pyramid of the Moon, both of which rival the Egyptian pyramids. Scattered throughout the Yucatan Peninsula are many well-preserved ruins of the ancient Mayan culture. Sites such as Uxmal, Chichen Itza, and Tulum will satisfy even the most discriminating ancient history buff. In order to find one of the most interesting places in the world to visit, a traveler needn't go far—only south of the border into Mexico.

# CHAPTER 8
# THE WAGES OF SIN

Over the past fifty plus years I have learned that, for me at least, crime doesn't pay. If I tell a falsehood, then it manages to come back and bite me where and when I least expect it. When I fudge the actual facts even slightly on my income tax; invariably something happens that requires my paying extra in some other category. For me a life of deception and crime is impossible. Apparently I simply was not cut out to be a finagler, a prevaricator, an equivocator, a lawbreaker or a rule bender of any sort. The following travel vignettes serve to prove my contention.

In 1966 when I was visiting Rome for the first time, I was particularly fascinated by the ancient history that lay all about me. I did a great deal of walking through historical sites like the Roman

Forum, up the Spanish Steps, all over the ruins of the Coliseum, through the Vatican City and around the Pantheon, to name a few. Also, I explored the Palatine Hill—one of the heights overlooking the Roman Forum. It was on that hill where the most famous of the emperors and senators chose to build their palaces.

At that time much of the Palatine had a fence around it and the officials at the gate charged a fee for tourists to wander among the various ruins. After hiking there from my hotel which was probably a half mile distant, I paid the admission charge and proceeded through the gate. As I went in I noticed several signs posted near the entrance and fortunately one of them was in English. In very large letters it said something like the following: "WARNING! DO NOT TAKE ANY ARTIFACTS LARGE OR SMALL FROM THE RUINS! VIOLATORS WILL BE PROSECUTED TO THE FULL EXTENT OF THE LAW! NO EXCEPTIONS!" Visions of tourists struggling with items such as stone altars or marble statuary crossed my mind. I could see them brazenly attempting to walk past the guards at the gate with their contraband. Such happenings seemed more comical than probable, however. I had very little room in my luggage for souvenirs, particularly anything large, so I ignored the sign and continued on my way. I felt that it simply didn't apply to me personally.

For the next several hours I enjoyed myself looking at the ruins of the different dwellings. My active imagination made them once again appear fully intact and in their former glory. In my mind's eye,

I saw historical figures like Marcus Aurelius, Brutus, Claudius and Augustus going about their daily lives in and about the buildings.

While walking through the remains of Julius Caesar's home, I particularly was taken with the intricate design of one of the tile floors. It was made of very small black stones contrasted with white stones and set in a complicated mosaic pattern. The tile floor was about all that remained of that room of the palace. In the dirt a little distance from the edge of the floor I saw several of the tiny tiles that had been dislodged from the pattern. I thought to myself, "What great souvenirs they would be to take back and show my history students at home!" Slyly, I looked around for guards and after seeing none, scooped up two of the tiles (a black one and a white one) and put them in my pocket.

My leisurely walk around the Palatine Hill continued for about another hour before I was ready to bring it to an end. As I neared the exit gate, suddenly I thought of two things. I remembered the warning sign by the entrance and at the same time thought of the two tiles resting in my pocket. I thought it probable I would be asked to empty my pockets as I left the park and my crime would be discovered. Visions of Roman newspaper headlines proclaiming (in Italian of course), "AMERICAN TEACHER ARRESTED FOR STEALING!" flashed through my mind.

What was I going to do? After thinking for a moment I came to a decision. Concealing myself behind a nearby tree, I removed the tiles from my pocket and stuffed them down the front of my trousers into my underwear. They made walking a bit uncomfortable but I reasoned, "At least I can empty my pockets without revealing the stolen tiles."

Stealthily, I came out from behind the tree and continued nervously on the way to the exit. All my fears and preparations, however, were in vain, for the gatekeepers paid me no heed as I exited the park and turned in the direction of my hotel. Apparently their only concerns were for the large items that the tourists might attempt to steal. Perhaps my original mental picture of visitors struggling with stone altars and marble statuary was not so far off the mark.

After returning to the hotel, I removed the "hot" items and put them in a dresser drawer for safe keeping until I left the city several days later. Those two tiles may still be in that dresser drawer for all I know. I promptly forgot where they were and consequently didn't pack them with my belongings when I left Rome. My little attempt at crime profited me not at all, except it gave me an amusing story to relate in my history classes as we studied the Roman Empire.

The "Big Island" of Hawaii provided the setting for another lesson in the "Crime Doesn't Pay School of Hard Knocks". A friend and I arranged to spend about a week on the islands in 1986. We began the first leg of the adventure by boarding a United Airlines flight at Tri-City Airport near Saginaw, Michigan and landing somewhat less than an hour later at Chicago's O'Hare International Airport. Because Illinois is on Central Standard Time, according to the clocks, we arrived in Chicago a few minutes before we took off from Saginaw. There we joined a non-stop Boeing 747 for the twelve hour trip to Honolulu on the island of Oahu. That flight across six time zones was my longest up to that point. It seemed interminable.

Finally, the plane approached the Honolulu Airport and while it descended we noticed that the landing strip was built on a man-made causeway out in Mamala Bay. As the 747 dropped to the narrow tarmac, it appeared almost as if we were landing on water because that was all we could see out the windows on either side. The pilot, however, brought us down safely and soon we were off the plane and being presented with the traditional Hawaiian greeting. Young and beautiful native girls placed leis around our necks and gave us a kiss on the cheek.

We had room reservations at a hotel on a canal not far from the city center and made that our headquarters as we explored the island. For the next couple of days we enjoyed all the sightseeing possibilities we could manage. We visited the Polynesian Cultural Center and watched their native dances at night by firelight. We took a half day bus tour around the entire island during which we saw our first triple rainbow and toured the Dole Pineapple factory. We visited the Bishop Museum of Polynesian studies and the Iolani Palace—the former home of Queen Liliuokalani. Previous to becoming a part of the United States, Hawaii was a monarchy ruled by a royal family. Offshore in Pearl Harbor we saw the U.S.S.

Arizona Memorial. That was one of the United States naval ships sunk by the Japanese during their December 7, 1941 bombing raid. As a result of that attack the U.S. declared war on the Axis powers the very next day.

One evening we attended a luau and ate food that had been wrapped in palm leaves and cooked in a pit of heated stones. We even managed to get a slight case of food poisoning from something we ate at Hamburger Mary's in downtown Honolulu. That didn't slow us down very much and we were soon on our way to further tourist attractions.

About midweek we scheduled a flight on Aloha Air, the local airline, and flew to the island of Hawaii—always referred to as the Big Island. Our small plane landed at Hilo, the only city on Hawaii, and there we boarded a bus to take us to several different tourist sites. The bus driver served as our guide. He was amazingly well informed about the island's geography, language, history and economics. During the next few hours, he gave us a fascinating and detailed short course about Hawaii. The driver's droll sense of humor kept us well entertained during the excursion.

Along the way to the volcanic peaks at the center of the Big Island, we made stops at Akaka Falls where we watched the narrow band of water fall over four hundred feet to the basin below and also at a macadamia farm where we sampled the products. Because the Hawaiian Islands were formed by volcanic action—and some of the volcanoes are still active—the state continues to grow in size.

There are two active volcanoes on the Big Island—Mauna Loa and Kilauea. Our destination was the Mauna Loa Caldera, or crater.

As we neared the caldera the driver became very serious in tone. He warned us that we must, under no circumstances, take any of the volcanic rock from the site. He told us that the goddess, Pele, had an extremely bad temper and did not tolerate the removal of anything from her home. We, of course, laughingly asked what the consequences were if that did happen. He became even more somber and related that many people in the past had ignored Pele's warnings and suffered dire consequences. We pressed him for details.

According to the driver, there are thousands of letters at the park headquarters that were written by previous visitors to the caldera. In the letters the people confessed to having removed lava rocks from the area. The writers went on to say that from that time on nothing but bad luck plagued them. Their investments dropped in value, their businesses failed, they contracted serious illnesses; and their children became insolent and disrespectful. Some of them developed chronic and unending headaches, others became crippled with arthritis. The list went on and on. At last, according to the driver, the people, one by one, came to the conclusion that their problems were caused by their having stolen rocks from Pele's home. He said that the letters of pain and remorse were invariably sent with a box containing the rocks that had been removed from the site. Some people even wrote follow-up letters claiming that their bad luck changed totally once the rocks were returned to their rightful home.

The driver's story convinced me that considering my past "crime doesn't pay" experiences; it would be a grave and foolish error for me to take anything from the volcanic site. Therefore, when I walked across the hot, smoking crust atop the caldera, I left everything exactly as I found it.

The most frightening of my brushes with those in power, whether they were governmental officials or the gods on high, occurred as a direct result of my second trip to Europe in 1966. On that occasion, I flew from Kennedy Airport near New York City to Copenhagen, Denmark on SAS (Scandinavian Air Service). The flight across the Atlantic was smooth, but it had one troubling aspect.

I was assigned the middle seat of three and on my left, next to the window, was a recent immigrant to the United States from Poland. He was a very pleasant fellow and we talked together during much of the flight. That was his first visit back to his homeland since immigrating and he was taking numerous gifts to his friends and relatives. Apparently, the bins overhead were all full because he had an oversized suitcase in front of his knees. It was so large that it extended into my small leg area as well. Consequently, all during the eight hour transatlantic flight both of us were forced to endure extremely cramped conditions. We were unable to change positions at all during the trip.

Today he would not have been allowed to have the suitcase with him as a carry-on because it couldn't possibly fit under the seat in front. Airline safety was a far different concern in 1966 from the present and so it was allowed at the time. Eventually, my ordeal was over when we landed at the Copenhagen Airport, but the Polish immigrant's discomfort would continue. Ahead of him still was another seven hundred and fifty mile flight to his Warsaw destination. I wished him *Bon Voyage* and with relief bade him goodbye.

My hotel was in the very center of Copenhagen on one side of the large City Hall Square. The square was a well landscaped park-like area with fountains, trees, benches and an occasional newspaper or magazine kiosk. The Danish people take full advantage of the warm weather during their short summers and often I saw fifty to sixty people enjoying the square and one another's company until late at night.

When I visit a city for the first time I try to do as much walking as I can in order to see the different sites. It seems that while walking I observe much more than I possibly could by riding in a taxi or on a bus. The day after my arrival in Copenhagen I attempted a hike to the city harbor. I learned that it was a long but enjoyable walk because I had to make my way through some of the older, narrow cobblestone streets. In as much as they are closed to automobile traffic, many of those ancient ways are almost like present-day malls. Eventually I made my slow way to the harbor where I found what I had been seeking. The Little Mermaid, a statue patterned after the main character from a Hans Christian Anderson fairy tale, sits on a rock out in the water and greets the ships as they come into the harbor. I had read about the statue and wanted to actually see it.

The next day I planned to visit Tivoli Gardens in the heart of Copenhagen. The day was balmy and I enjoyed the twenty minute stroll to the park. Tivoli Gardens is one of the oldest amusement parks in the world. It covers twenty acres near the center of the city and has restaurants, a variety of rides, games of chance, fortune tellers, bingo parlors, musical entertainments, ice cream shops and many other snack food vendors. On that particular day the spectators were treated to a precision marching band, with handsome blue uniforms and lots of gold braid, which performed its maneuvers in an open field on the park grounds.

While returning to my hotel from the park, I happened past the display window of a small bookstore on one of the downtown streets. Idly, I glanced at the books on display in the window. Suddenly, I halted and did a double take. There, displayed openly along one of the main thoroughfares of the city, was explicit pictorial pornography! At that time, in 1966, American booksellers, if they sold pornography at all, had it secreted under the counter and well out of sight. In fact, it was against the law to have it available, so all sales had to be transacted covertly. I was amazed at the more liberal Danish attitudes toward the subject, and <u>very</u> interested.

I entered the bookshop and glanced around at the displays. There were best-selling novels, classics, poetry books, how-to books, self-help books, biographies and lots of pornography. I wandered about, made a few selections and then looked for the cash register. The cashier, who was a female, said something in Danish which I'm sure was the equivalent of, "May I help you?" Immediately, I became tongue-tied and couldn't utter a word. I was attempting to buy explicit pornography and the only cashier was a woman. The women I knew in America didn't even read that sort of thing, let alone sell it publicly. It crossed my mind to put the books down and escape the premises, but I didn't. Red faced, I gathered up my courage and handed the books to her. Nonchalantly she rang up the sales, accepted my money and gave me change; as though it were an everyday occurrence. Which, of course, for her it was.

At this point I'm going to move this story ahead in time and to another location. About three weeks after the incident in Copenhagen, I landed at the Detroit Airport after flying in from London with a short stopover at Kennedy Airport in New York City. A friend who had offered to pick me up met me at the flight gate in Detroit. I proceeded to the baggage claim and waited for my luggage to appear. One of the suitcases came out quickly, but the other never showed up. I gave my claim ticket to the official there and he indicated he would put out an alert for the bag. He suggested that I go on my way and he would call me as soon as he heard anything. The next afternoon he did call me at my Saginaw home with this strange news. My other suitcase mistakenly had been put on a flight to Iceland rather than on the correct one to New York. So the result was that my suitcase had been to Iceland but I had never been there.

Approximately a week later I received a call from a U.S. State Department official telling me that my suitcase was at the city bus station in Saginaw and I could come down and pick it up. It seems they wanted me present while they opened it and checked it through customs. At that point I remembered the pornography from Copenhagen and also remembered that I had packed it in that suitcase. I panicked. Once again I could see ugly headlines in the local newspaper prominently featuring my name linked to illegally bringing pornography into the country. I berated myself for ever buying it in the first place. Why, oh why, did I commit such a foolhardy act?

Nervously, I drove to the bus station and presented myself to the official there. My knees were shaking as he located the suitcase and proceeded to open it. At least the contraband books weren't on the top but were hidden somewhere below. Perfunctorily he felt around the interior of the suitcase, closed it and handed it to me. He also had me sign a receipt form. Whew! I was saved by his carelessness and lack of dedication to his job. After that exceptionally close call, I vowed never again to purchase anything abroad that had even the vaguest hint of being illegal.

Yes, indeed, for me the simple fact remains; "crime doesn't pay"!

# CHAPTER 9
# CALIFORNIA BOUND

A four thousand mile trip to California and back in a 1950's MG sports car caused the abrupt end of one of my early adult friendships. The friend, Nick Cook, and I had known one another for three years, but the relationship simply wasn't able to withstand the forced togetherness inherent in such a motor trip. The trip only lasted about three weeks, but before it was over it seemed as though it encompassed an entire miserable lifetime. This is the story of the initial rise and later decline and fall of our friendship.

Most of my required two-year army hitch was spent near Columbia, South Carolina, at Fort Jackson. I taught typing at the Supply School there. The school was an integral part of the second eight weeks basic training for all recruits entering the Quartermaster

Corps. I lived in a barracks and had my meals in a mess hall which were part of the Regimental Headquarters unit. The entire regiment was under the command of an army colonel.

One evening shortly after I arrived at Fort Jackson, I met Nick when we happened to share a table at dinner. We introduced ourselves and during our conversation learned that we had much in common. Both of us were from small towns—he was a Pennsylvanian and I was a Michigander. Both of us were recent college graduates and had taught secondary school for a year prior to being drafted into the army. Each of us had brought a book to dinner so it was apparent that we had that interest in common, too. We learned that our rooms were in the same barracks building. Later, we discovered that each of us was interested in theatre and acting as well. During the next year and a half, Nick and I became good friends. Our tours of duty ended at approximately the same time and we were discharged from the army in the summer of 1958.

After our return to civilian life and teaching, Nick and I corresponded with one another through the next school year. In our letters back and forth we each confessed to having a desire to visit California. Therefore we made plans to go there on a driving trip during the following summer vacation. Nick had purchased a new MG sports car and offered his vehicle for the drive. We agreed to share the expenses of the trip. The plan called for Nick to drive to Michigan late in June, pick me up and then we would head for the Far West from that starting point.

Nick pulled into my hometown at the appointed time, but he arrived there with bad news. He confessed that he was short of money and didn't have enough to pay for his half of the cost of the trip. Small town teacher's salaries in the late 1950's were very low. Mine was less than $4,000 for the entire year; therefore I had no extra money for making him a loan. In fact, I had taken a part time job that summer with the local fair board in order to insure my being able to afford the California trip. We talked about the problem at length and at first saw no solution other than canceling the excursion.

Because my hometown of Vassar was very small—only 3,500 inhabitants—I knew the bank president, Gordon Glazier, personally. On a hunch, I made an appointment with Gordon and explained the entire situation to him. He seemed very sympathetic and readily agreed to give me the money on a signature loan which I could repay in small monthly installments during the next school year.

With that problem behind us, we happily loaded the MG and set out for California. MG sports cars of the 1950's were miniscule in size. The passenger compartment comprised two narrow bucket seats and there was no back seat at all. The trunk was just large enough to hold two small suitcases with no room to spare. We packed very lightly and made plans to stop regularly at Laundromats along the way to keep us in clean clothing.

The weather that June and July was beautiful and perfect for driving. The days were sunny and nearly cloudless while the humidity remained low. We made rapid progress through the Midwest and crossed Michigan, Illinois, Iowa and part of Nebraska in a little over two days. Because the Interstate Highway System was still only in its planning stages in 1959, we traveled on state highways and, when possible, we by-passed the larger cities along the way.

In Colorado we intended to visit another army friend, George Barnett. After George's discharge from the service, he took a job as a telegrapher for the railroad and was assigned to a station in northeastern Colorado in the tiny village of Eckley. The town had only a little over a hundred inhabitants at the time and served as an oasis in the horizon to horizon grassland of that corner of the state. After a number of trials and errors we eventually located the little settlement which was not far from the north fork of the Republican River. The village consisted of a restaurant, a six-occupant rooming house across the road, a combination general store and gas station, a handful of houses, the small railroad station where George worked, and very little else. It boasted a few scrawny weather-beaten trees which comprised all the landscaping other than the ubiquitous dry, yellow grass.

Nick and I arrived in mid-week so we spent a couple of days there until George was free on Friday evening for the long Fourth of July weekend. The three of us planned to go to Denver where George had an apartment in his parents' house. While in Eckley, all of us stayed at the small rooming house and were charged $2.00

per day. The place was hardly luxurious in its appointments. The ramshackle structure was built of rough-sawn boards nailed to a two by four wood frame. Cracks between the boards admitted light as well as many varieties of grassland insects. Our beds were small army-surplus cots wide enough for one person, if he didn't roll too far when turning over—otherwise he would end up on the uncarpeted floor boards. A bare bulb with a pull chain, hanging from the center of the wood ceiling, provided the only artificial light. There was no plumbing in the rooming house; therefore we used the privy out back at night. During the day when the restaurant across the road was open for business we could use the flush-type toilet there. The restaurant and rooming house were owned and operated by the same family. We whiled away the next couple of days by exploring the rather barren countryside.

The following weekend George, Nick and I made the rounds of the nightspots in Denver and during the daylight hours admired the Rocky Mountain scenery west of the city. We also visited the historic mining town of Golden just beyond the metropolitan area, in addition to the nearby Red Rock natural amphitheater. George proudly showed off his home city to us and we enjoyed his company and his hospitality.

On July 4th, we left George in Denver and aimed the MG westward to continue toward California. About sixty miles into the Rockies we crossed one of the highest of the mountain passes at a place called Loveland. With an elevation of nearly 12.000 feet above sea level, Loveland Pass usually has snow all year around. That year was no exception. Previously neither of us had ever seen snow on the Fourth of July, and excitedly we stopped to frolic in it. We even had a snowball fight on the slope near where we parked the car.

Beyond Loveland Pass the highway took us westward to the famous skiing hamlet of Vail lying in what is likely one of the most beautiful mountain valleys in the world. There we stopped to window-shop in the very expensive and trendy stores that made up its downtown area. From the streets of the business district we enviously gazed up at palatial multi-million dollar homes clinging to the sides of the mountains which formed the valley walls.

Perhaps forty miles west of the ski resort, the highway joined the Colorado River Valley and we followed its meanderings the rest of the way to the Utah border. Enroute we passed through the city of Grand Junction where the Gunnison River joins the Colorado River. That city was given its name when the Colorado River was still called the Grand River. In Utah we turned south, by-passed the Grand Canyon, and quickly covered the distance to Arizona where we joined old Route 66 for the rest of the trip to Los Angeles and Hollywood.

In Hollywood we planned to visit an acquaintance of mine, Gage Clark, an actor who originally hailed from my hometown in Michigan. Gage, though he never became a star, earned a good living doing small parts in movies and television. During the early part of his acting career, he even had a few stage credits in Broadway shows. I met Gage the previous spring when he spent some time in Vassar settling his mother's estate. He invited me to visit him on our drive to California and offered to show us around Hollywood.

Until that part of the trip, Nick had been his usual happy, carefree self. We both enjoyed the places we visited and the people we met. Soon, however, signs appeared that we were becoming travel weary. The strain of nearly constant driving in an extremely cramped auto and being thrown together so much of the time started to cause serious friction between us. We began to snap at one another for little or no reason. Nick became moody and given to long periods of near silence. When that happened, the only sound emanating from him was the grinding of his teeth against one another. Together we decided that it was time to forsake California and head toward our homes.

The next two thousand five hundred mile leg of our journey was pure Hell. We both were running short of money which required our staying in fleabag hotels and motels. We were verbally vicious to one another—each blaming the other for the poor quality of the rooms. Nick was hyper-critical of everything I said or did; consequently I lapsed into long, black silences that were louder than screams. The tiny MG seemed to get smaller and more confining each mile we traveled.

Though Nick and I, on that return trip, drove through some of the most beautiful mountain and desert scenery found on the North

American continent, we didn't appreciate any of it. The landscape was merely something to by-pass during our tediously slow, mile after endless mile, homeward journey. Sometimes an entire hour would pass with neither of us saying a word. We were very unhappy travelers and anxious to forsake one another's company.

Late one evening, after what seemed an eternity, we crossed the Indiana border into Michigan. I thought, "At last our long ordeal is coming to an end!" One issue however, still faced us—one which would cause further discord. A little after two o'clock in the morning the gasoline indicator was on empty and we were about twenty-five or thirty miles from Vassar. Nick asked me if there were any all-night gas stations in the vicinity. I guessed that there probably were a few but didn't know for certain. Each time we approached one that I thought might be open, we found it closed. Meanwhile the gas indicator inched ever lower. Nick became very agitated and appeared to blame me for the stations' short hours of operation.

Eventually, we limped into Vassar on mere fumes and parked in the lot behind my apartment building. Wearily, we grabbed our bags and made our tired way up the stairs. We fell into bed and immediately were asleep. I slept fitfully all night because my head was filled with a hideous nightmare in which we were still driving cross-country and making no progress whatsoever. I must have traveled a thousand imaginary miles that night!

The next morning our moods had improved not a whit, thus we were very cool toward one another. Thankfully, Nick wished to be on his way to Pennsylvania as soon as possible, so I was able to bid him goodbye shortly after we were out of bed. Never had I been so eager to see the last of a friend.

The summer ended and I became busy with the fall start-up of school. Several months passed and I heard nothing from Nick. I felt no great desire to continue our friendship, but did have serious concerns about the borrowed money which I had loaned to him. At the time we had made no contract, nor had we agreed upon a repayment timetable. In the meantime, I was required to make monthly payments on the loan to the bank.

Shortly before Christmas, when I thought he had had plenty of time to begin repaying the loan, I wrote to Nick. In the letter I suggested that he send me a small amount each month; and also reminded him that the bank expected regular payments from me. About a month later I received a cryptic letter from Nick saying that he recently had a number of unexpected expenses, but would begin repaying me. Included in the letter was a check for $10.00. Thereafter, a check for the same amount, with no note included, arrived in the mail each month. He repaid the face value of the loan, after deducting some automobile expenses, but included no interest or thanks for bailing him out in a time of need.

I have heard nothing from Nick during the more than forty-three years that have elapsed since then. It is often said that one never should loan money to family or friends because it surely will cause friction in the family or the loss of the friendship. In my estimation the loan was only partially to blame for the demise of our friendship. More importantly, I think it was destroyed by our close proximity over an extended period of time on the California trip. Apparently the relationship simply was not strong enough to survive the strains and pressures it had faced.

# CHAPTER 10
# "QUEUING UP" IN THE ORIENT

"Why doesn't this line move forward?" I mused impatiently to myself as I waited my turn to use one of the airplane's restrooms. After twenty-five minutes had elapsed, I finally made it to the corner near the head of the line and then was able to see what was causing the long delay. Asians, who made up the bulk of the passengers on that particular flight, approached the line to the restroom and simply edged in near the front of the queue, totally ignoring the rare but polite protests from the few Westerners who obediently were awaiting their turns. Later I learned that such actions by Asians were far from unusual. In fact, during the three weeks I spent in the Orient, I discovered that it was the norm rather than the exception.

Westerners are taught from a very young age to wait their turn in line. They may do so grudgingly but on the whole they do it anyway. Rarely does anyone try to cut ahead of others. It is my observation that Orientals are trained from an equally young age to do just the opposite. They will push ahead of others whenever and wherever they are able to do so. They force themselves in front with no sign of embarrassment or chagrin. In fact they accomplish it with such adroitness and with such a sense of savoir faire that they usually get away with it unscathed.

In 1996 I was invited by my nephew, Daniel, and his wife, Jennifer, to visit them in what was then the English colony of Hong Kong. Hong Kong has since then become a province of the Republic of China. Daniel was teaching linguistics and English at the university there and Jennifer was a librarian at the same institution. They had lived in Hong Kong for four or five years and, because of the distances involved, had few visitors from the United States. Consequently they were eager to see a familiar face from home. That was about ten years after I had retired from teaching and thought that the trip would be an excellent opportunity for me to renew acquaintances with Daniel and Jennifer and, as a distinct bonus, to see a part of the Orient as well.

A friend drove me to Detroit where I boarded the Boeing 747 at the Detroit Metro Airport. From there the Northwest Airlines flight flew non-stop to Japan. I had a window seat giving me an opportunity to observe the change from day to night and back to day once more. We boarded at about mid-morning and as we flew westward across the time zones it became progressively earlier. Somewhere over the Pacific Ocean we crossed the International Date Line where we lost a day. Therefore, we ended up landing at mid-morning on the second day after our departure from Detroit. Though we had flown only twelve hours by the clock, according to the calendar a day and a half had elapsed before we landed. Our destination in Japan was the Narita Airport which serves the Tokyo metropolitan area. It was during that flight which crossed eleven time zones, the restroom incident occurred that I described above. The unpleasant experience helped make the trip seem even longer than it actually was.

To amuse myself during the long airplane ride, I studied the flight map in the complimentary Northwest Airlines Magazine located in the seat pocket. I thought that it was especially interesting that on a direct flight from Detroit to Tokyo one doesn't cross the Pacific Ocean anywhere near the Hawaiian Islands which are near the center of the body of water. Instead it follows a path far north of that. The shortest distance between the two cities crosses northern Canada, Alaska, several islands off the eastern coast of China and finally the northern Japanese island of Hokkaido before it ends on the island of Honshu where Tokyo is situated. That path is called "a great circle route" and when one stretches a string from the two points on a globe the string will cross those locations. If the pilot were to steer the airplane across the Pacific Ocean near its center he would be flying hundreds of miles out of his way though on most maps it looks as though it is a straight line. That optical illusion is the direct result of all flat maps being inaccurate due to the fact that they are representing a curved surface—the earth.

In Japan, during the hour-long layover before my connecting flight to Hong Kong, I was subjected to another example of the Asian disdain for standing in line. Even though I was not leaving the airport and would be flying out in a short time, I was still required to go through a security check. I located the security checkpoint and dutifully joined the end of the line in front of the official there. It was a long line and one which moved interminably slowly. From my vantage point near the end of it I was able to observe the exact reason for its snail-like progress. Person after person joined the line near its front rather than at the rear. No one made any fuss or verbal objection to those encroachments as far as I could tell. Of course all the conversation was in Japanese and I had no idea what was being said, but no one appeared to be upset except me. I was furious! However, because I was a foreigner and a stranger to the customs of the country, I bit my tongue and said not a word of objection. Consequently I spent the entire hour-long layover in that line for the security check. When at last I reached the checkpoint and passed through it, I had only minutes to locate the departure gate and catch my flight to Hong Kong.

Four hours later we flew over the lights of Hong Kong and landed at the Kai Tak Airport which was situated on a man-made peninsula extending out from the area of the colony called Kowloon. Kowloon is connected on the north to the mainland of China. Daniel and Jennifer met me at the arrival gate. I was exhausted from spending the past twenty hours on airplanes or in airports; therefore I was very happy to see them. We located a taxi and shortly were on our way to the university apartment house where they lived. We had to cross Victoria Harbor to the island of Hong Kong. There are two main routes drivers may use to get from Kowloon to the island. Our taxi driver chose to take the faster one—the Cross-Harbor Tunnel—a mile and a half underground route that crosses beneath the waters of Victoria Harbor. The slower route would have been aboard one of the auto ferries that makes frequent crossings between the two locations.

Over the next few days Daniel and Jennifer showed me a few of the interesting attractions in Hong Kong. The overwhelming impression I had of the city was that it virtually teemed with vehicles and humanity. Nearly six million people made their homes in the colony at the time of my visit. The streets were crowded day and night with honking autos, smelly buses and noisy trucks—the sidewalks were solid streams of pedestrians; most of whom had cell phones glued to their ears. Many modern skyscrapers dotted the island because land was very limited and the only logical direction to expand was up. The restaurants were so crowded that there was always a long wait for a table. It is said that Hong Kong has the best shopping in the world. All the many and varied stores seemed to be filled with customers from opening time until closing time.

We had one quiet respite from the masses of humanity and the fast-paced business momentum when we visited the Zoological Park in the very heart of the overcrowded city. There we walked from the noisy, traffic infested streets into the quiet haven of the park where the only sounds were those made by the birds as they flitted about the net-enclosed aviary. I noticed that many natives regularly used the park as a quiet retreat to sit for a moment to read or merely for contemplation. It served as a subdued oasis in an otherwise frantic maelstrom of activity.

Victoria Peak is the highest hill overlooking Hong Kong Harbor. The route to the crest is precipitous and the steepest funicular railway in the world, called the Peak Tram, takes passengers up and down regularly. My nephew and I boarded the tramcar at the lower terminus near the Zoological Park and rode nearly two thousand feet to the top. Enroute we passed five intermediate stations before reaching the upper terminus. From that height we could see the entire thirty square miles of Hong Kong Island. Off to the north, across Victoria Harbor, Kowloon was also clearly visible, as well as a part of the border with mainland China. I was particularly impressed with the many, many container ships which were plying their ways in and out of the crowded waterway. Hong Kong is one of the busiest harbors in the world.

The following weekend Daniel and I had reservations on Dragon Airlines to fly from Hong Kong to Beijing, China, for a three-day visit. At the airport I observed yet another example of the Asian unwillingness to obediently stand in line and take their legitimate turn when it came. Daniel and I arrived very early at the airport; therefore we were first in line for boarding the small jet that would fly us to China. Soon other passengers arrived and they immediately began wide flanking movements to get around us in an attempt to board before we did. Daniel, who had lived there for several years, was determined not to let that happen. He had us spread our luggage out each side of us in order to present a wide front to the would-be usurpers. When one of them would make a move to pass us, we would make a counter move to stop him. That happened several times and eventually they realized that we were determined that they would not prevail. Consequently they gave up and we were able to keep our positions at the head of the line. Our success gave me a real feeling of accomplishment because, up to then, I had always been the loser in the test of wills with the Orientals. Revenge was very, very sweet!

Our flight to Beijing lasted a little over two hours. We took a taxi from the Beijing Airport on a modern four-lane divided highway. We were quickly deposited at the Beijing Hilton where we would be staying while in the city.

My preconceived notion that Chinese cities were backward metropolitan areas was soon destroyed when I took a really good look at the hotel. It was sumptuous and supremely luxurious in every detail. The large lobby was swathed in highly polished hardwoods and thick area carpets covered marble floors. My sixth-floor room had one of the most luxurious bathrooms I have ever seen. There were gold fittings, three colors of marble covered nearly every surface and there was a large, glassed in shower in addition to a ceramic tub. Piles of fluffy towels rested on the shelves. The window of the hotel room provided a spectacular view of the huge city. The room contained two double beds, a well-stocked refrigerator, a safe and many other refinements.

Included with the price of the room was a bounteous breakfast. Each morning seven or eight tables were set up at one end of the dining room where foods of many different nationalities were presented for the taking. While we were having breakfast, a pianist entertained us with classical music. If we chose to have lunch or dinner at the hotel, we were treated to a string quartet playing other classical selections.

Daniel and I managed to squeeze an impressive amount of sightseeing into the next several days. We visited the Forbidden City, which was the home of the early Chinese emperors. We walked across Tiananmen Square in the city's center. That was the site of the 1989 student demonstrations that were televised worldwide. I recall watching a newscast and seeing one young unarmed student bravely facing down a military tank in the square. The tank driver eventually gave way and turned aside while the student continued his protest unharmed. Also we took a taxi north of the city and walked on a portion of the fifteen hundred mile long Great Wall of China. We visited the Summer Palace of the emperors in the southeast corner of the city. And, finally, we walked through the old commercial part of Beijing, going down little meandering alleys lined with tiny shops selling a wide variety of items. Those small business places contrasted dramatically with the grand multi-storied department stores in the newer business district near our hotel.

Monday morning came all too soon and it found us on the return flight to Hong Kong; where we were met by Jennifer. She was unable to make the trip with us because of being scheduled to work at the university library that weekend. However, the following weekend, my last of the visit, the three of us took a jetfoil ferry across the forty miles of water separating Hong Kong from the tiny Portuguese colony of Macao. Macao, like Hong Kong, has since become a province of the Republic of China.

Back in Hong Kong I was treated to yet another incident of the Oriental aversion to standing in lines. In this case the result was far different that those I've described up to now. A few days into my stay with Daniel and Jennifer, I ran short of Hong Kong dollars and had to get some travelers checks cashed at a bank. Inside the bank, lines had formed in front of each of the teller's windows. I chose the shortest one of the lines and joined the end. In passing I noticed that the line was made up entirely of Westerners who obediently were waiting their turns with the teller.

Before I had been there more than a few minutes, an Asian entered the bank. He confidently walked to the head of our line and, when the person being served was finished, he stepped in front of the teller, fully expecting to be waited on next. Not so! The teller peered around him and asked the next one in line if she could help him. I thought to myself, "Bully for the teller! She was striking a forceful blow for the underdog!" The teller totally ignored the line crasher standing before her. It was almost as if he didn't even exist. Eventually he was forced to the side and left the line. I didn't watch what he did next, so am not aware if he managed to crash another line or not, but hopefully he was unable to do so. That little incident went a long way toward improving my overall attitude toward Asians. I thought, "Perhaps some of them _do_ have a sense of fair play, after all."

# CHAPTER 11
# ACCIDENTS AND NEAR MISSES

What does a teacher-driver do when his school bus stops dead miles from town while traversing a huge mud puddle that is both longer and wider than the vehicle itself? That was the dilemma that faced me when I was about five miles east of Vassar, Michigan on a graveled country road during the very rainy spring of 1956. No matter what I did in an attempt to start the bus again, nothing worked. The engine was totally dead. Some of the school children, who were my passengers, began getting a bit antsy so I knew that something had to be done and sooner would be better than later.

That incident occurred well before the proliferation of cell phones so that was not an option open to me. Therefore, forfeiting all my newly acquired teacher dignity, I took off my highly polished shoes, removed my socks and rolled my pant legs up well above my ankles. Carrying my shoes and socks, I waded through the cold water to the edge of the road. Fortunately, there happened to be a farm nearby. After replacing socks and shoes on wet feet, I sloshed my way to the house and asked if I could use their phone. The lady of the house gave me permission and I called the bus garage. The dispatcher agreed to send out a tow truck in addition to a substitute school bus to rescue us.

When help arrived, I learned that the battery in the school bus had fallen out of its old, rusty support harness. It had pulled its electrodes loose and was lying in the middle of the mud puddle under the vehicle. Little wonder that all my efforts to restart the engine came to naught. Several hours later and somewhat worse for wear, I finally made it back to my apartment in town after the substitute bus had dropped the remaining children at their various homes.

As a low paid beginning teacher at Vassar High School who needed to supplement his income, I had agreed to drive school bus both mornings and afternoons. My total salary for that year was $2,800, but with the added money for driving I earned the grand sum of $3,200 that year. The low salary had convinced me to take on the added responsibility of bus driving in addition to teaching..

That story describes only one of the accidents or near misses that have plagued me during my more than fifty-five year driving career. Some incidents were scary and some were amusing, but all of them had the potential for being serious. I count myself fortunate to be numbered among those who never have been injured in a driving accident.

A phenomenon called "black ice" was the culprit that caused one of my more frightening accidents. On a dark December Friday evening in 1978, while living in Midland, Michigan, I was driving south on I-75 toward Detroit where I planned to spend the weekend. No snow had fallen as yet that year, the highway was clear and I was moving along at the posted speed of sixty miles per hour. About half way between Flint and Detroit, just past the Clarkston Exit, I came over the rise of a small hill. Immediately after passing the crest, I felt the car begin to yaw and swerve due to the invisible ice on the road's surface. My compensating turn into the swerve only caused the car to veer in the opposite direction. After a couple of sashays back and forth I found myself facing in the direction from which I had come, and moving backward down the sloping highway.

Suddenly a pair of headlights crested the hill aiming directly toward my car as it careened backward. The approaching auto—a large Cadillac—was traveling much faster than my tiny American Motors Pacer and the two vehicles collided mid-hill. The collision caused my vehicle to veer to the south and eventually it ended up with its back end in a ditch at the side of the highway. The Cadillac came to a stop on the roadside not far away.

Unhurt, I got out of my vehicle and made my way to the Cadillac in order to see if its occupants were okay. The driver said that

119

he, his wife and elderly mother-in-law seemed to be fine though understandably, badly shaken by the incident. The man used his portable phone to call the police station. Shortly thereafter several police cars, an ambulance and two wreckers appeared at the scene of the accident. When the paperwork was completed the officers gave me a ride to the next exit where there was a gas station. I used the station's pay phone to call my sister and brother-in-law, Joanne and Richard, who, fortunately for me, lived nearby in Clarkston. They picked me up and as we drove back toward the Clarkston Exit on the freeway we passed my crumpled Pacer being hauled behind a wrecker.

I never made it to Detroit that weekend as Joanne and Richard drove me home to Midland the next day. Later that week I learned that both the Pacer and the Cadillac were totaled in the accident. As a result, I spent a few days doing a lot of walking and asking for rides from friends while making arrangements to buy another vehicle as a replacement for the wrecked one. Ever since that incident, I always think of that dark Friday night each time I pass over the crest of that hill on I-75 near the Clarkston Exit on the way to Detroit.

The most tragic of my near misses occurred on the freeway between Saginaw and Flint in central Lower Michigan. My companion and I came out of it unscathed but it had deadly consequences for five others. On a Saturday afternoon in the summer of 1995, we were driving to Flint where we were to attend a birthday party. The sun was shining, the pavement was dry and visibility was perfect. The Saturday afternoon traffic was very heavy and all three lanes in both directions were nearly filled with automobiles.

We had almost reached the trucker's weigh station just south of the Bridgeport Exit and were moving along at the speed limit of seventy miles per hour, when two Corvettes passed us going well over the speed limit. My estimate would be that the racing vehicles were attaining speeds from ninety-five to one hundred miles per hour. I was driving in the lane near the median, and the first Corvette, with the second one tail-gating it, passed me on the right, cut directly in front of my car and almost immediately went out of control. The speeding vehicle turned at a right angle, skidded backward through the median and started across the oncoming lane of traffic where it was struck by a northbound car. The impact of the collision threw the Corvette onto the roadside at the opposite side of the highway where it burst into flames. Meanwhile the second Corvette drove on unaffected.

All traffic came to a stop and many of us left our cars by the side of the road and raced back in order to see what could be done for those involved in the horrendous accident. We soon learned that little or nothing could be done. The Corvette was totally engulfed in flames and obviously, if the lone occupant survived the collision, then he burned to death immediately afterward. The northbound vehicle which had struck the Corvette; was terribly damaged and the driver and his three children were killed in the impact.

Later we learned that the drivers of the two Corvettes, both of whom were young men, had spent the day at the Bay City boat races where they began drinking heavily. After the conclusion of the races when they were on their way south along the freeway toward home, they began racing one another. That bit of foolishness led to the fiery death of one of them as well as the tragic demise of four additional people including three innocent children.

After viewing the fiery inferno, the two of us retrieved our car and glumly continued on our way toward Flint and the birthday party. The grotesque incident cast a pall over us and we had little stomach for taking part in the festivities we encountered there.

In 1997, my friend, Ron, and I moved from Michigan to the city of Albuquerque, New Mexico, in order to take advantage of the warm, dry desert climate found there. It was a good move and one that we have never regretted since. Our home is on the newly developed west side of the city across the Rio Grande from both the downtown and the old town areas. Bordering the northwest edge of Albuquerque is a large suburb, called Rio Rancho, with probably 60,000 inhabitants. Rio Rancho was the site of yet another unusual auto accident that could have had dire consequences for the two of us.

Ron and I often ate our evening meals at various restaurants in and around Albuquerque. On that particular day we had chosen one of the many eating establishments lining highway NM 528—the main north and south street through Rio Rancho. By the time we

122

were finished with dinner and were on our way back home it had become dark.

There is a traffic light where Twenty-First Street crosses highway NM 528 just south of the giant Intel Corporation buildings. As we approached the intersection the traffic light turned red and we pulled to a stop. We waited there for the light to change so we could proceed. In a flash we were struck from behind! The backs of our seats broke from the impact and we found ourselves lying flat with bits of glass from the back window raining down upon us. The force of the collision drove our vehicle through the intersection and when it came to a stop it was in the left lane south of Twenty-First Street. Fortunately there were no autos crossing the intersection when we careened through it or we could have been killed.

After we righted ourselves and were untangled from the seatbelts, we got out of the car to see what had struck us and to survey the damage it had caused. We learned that the culprit was a large pick-up truck driven by a young man with his girl friend as a passenger. He claimed that he saw our vehicle sitting at the intersection in front of him and attempted to stop, but his brakes failed, causing the collision. I think that the more likely story was that he was paying more attention to the girl than the road ahead and when at last he saw our car it was too late to prevent the heavy pick-up from colliding with it.

Ironically, the pick-up incurred little or no damage, but Ron's auto—a Ford Probe less than a year old—was a total loss.

Apparently the frame was so badly distorted from the impact that the vehicle could not be repaired. Both of us came away from the incident with severe headaches and a few days of backaches but, other than those minor complaints, we were physically unhurt. The more serious damage we suffered was emotional. For months afterward, any time either of us came to a stop at a traffic light we looked behind us to see if any vehicles were there. We panicked whenever approaching cars seemed to be closing the distance too quickly. Eventually the young man's insurance paid for Ron's car, and the two of us each were awarded $3,000 for "pain and suffering" caused from the accident.

Only four years later Ron and I were involved in the most spectacular near miss that either one of us could ever have dreamed up in our wildest flights of imagination. During the early part of the summer in 2002 we made a driving trip back to Michigan for a ten-day visit. The days flew by and in what seemed like no time, we were ready to begin the return trip to New Mexico. We left Midland, which had been our headquarters during the visit, very early on a Sunday morning. As was our habit when driving between Michigan and New Mexico, we stopped for breakfast at a small restaurant on highway M-46 near the town of Breckenridge. After eating we followed that route west to the junction of U.S 27 and there turned south toward Lansing.

The day was overcast and the pavement was wet from a drizzle of rain that was falling. When we had driven ten or fifteen miles south of the intersection, we neared the bridge that crosses the Maple River. Ron was driving and I was in the passenger seat. Suddenly, just before we were at the bridge, he looked in the rear view mirror and yelled, "Oh, my God!" As I watched out Ron's side of the car, another vehicle sped past us on the left. Just a short distance beyond our car the passer lost control of his vehicle and it turned to the right directly in our path. We barely missed the car as it leapt onto the right shoulder and turned in the same direction from which it had come. We bypassed the auto on the bridge and then as I watched out the back window it once again crossed the highway and came to a jolting stop in the median. The runaway vehicle had made a complete circle around our moving car and never even grazed it!

Upon reflection we came to the conclusion that the driver, a man in his early twenties, had fallen asleep at the wheel with his cruise control engaged. Apparently he awakened just before he would have hit the rear of our car. His wide-eyed, frightened stare as he rapidly overtook us was what Ron had observed in the rear view mirror before yelling, "Oh, my God!" Then the young man cramped the wheel to the left and went around our vehicle before he lost control of his car and completed the circle of ours.

We surmised that he was a Michigan State University student who had been partying and drinking all night in Mount Pleasant and was on his way back to East Lansing when he went to sleep. His answers were totally incoherent when we and the others who stopped to help attempted to question him. As he sat in his car in the highway median, he reeked of alcohol and seemed barely able to focus his eyes. He had the appearance of being very drunk and certainly in no proper condition to be driving a car.

Eventually the police appeared on the scene and took charge of the situation thus Ron and I were free to go. Nervously, we returned to our car and continued on the route toward New Mexico. That evening we stopped to spend the night at a motel in central Missouri. After much tossing and turning, I was finally able to drop off to sleep but dreamed the entire night about the frightening events of the day.

No matter how you view them, automobile accidents are traumatic events. Even the near misses can be equally as frightening as those in which an actual collision occurs.

# CHAPTER 12
# THE VERY TALL LADY

The year was 1999 and I was traveling from my home in Albuquerque, New Mexico to Saginaw, Michigan. I had been invited to attend my fiftieth year high school class reunion and was on the second leg of the journey to my childhood hometown of Vassar, a small city located a few miles east of Saginaw. Earlier that morning I had boarded a Northwest Airlines flight in Albuquerque and it had landed at the Minneapolis-St. Paul Airport. I made my way across the huge concourse and located the gate for my connecting flight to Saginaw. There I sat down to wait for the boarding process to begin. To while away the time until the take off, I amused myself by working the daily crossword puzzle in the newspaper.

During one of the times when I looked up from the puzzle, I noticed a lady joining the group waiting for the plane. She was the tallest woman I had ever seen. The lady had to be well over six feet because she literally towered over my height of five foot nine inches. Every one in the waiting area took note of her. Apparently she was used to that reaction because she ignored all the rude stares and quietly waited for the airplane's arrival.

After half an hour had elapsed, the boarding process began. I joined the line and went down the ramp to the aircraft and located my seat. A few minutes later the lady boarded the airplane and took the vacant seat next to mine. We nodded to one another as we buckled our seat belts and settled in for the trip. I had realized immediately with my first glimpse of her in the airport waiting area that there was something definitely familiar about her face, but I couldn't place her or think of her name. As we sat there for a few moments awaiting the take-off, I searched my mind for who she was and pondered why I seemed to recognize her. For the time being no inspiration came to me about her identity. Still the nagging thought remained that I knew her from somewhere.

The pilot taxied the aircraft away from the exit gate and proceeded across the tarmac toward the take-off runway. There the plane gathered speed and just as its wheels lifted off I realized who the tall lady was. Surprisingly, at that very instant she and I both turned to one another and spoke simultaneously. She said, "Aren't you Jerry?" And I said, "Aren't you Jim?" Our answers to the questions were very different. Mine was, "Yes, I am." But hers was, "I used to be, but now I'm Cheryl."

I had been introduced to Jim some twenty years previously while living and teaching in Saginaw. At the time that I met him he was still married and was the father of three children. Jim went to some of the same parties I attended, we had many friends in common and often we would run across one another at several Saginaw nightclubs that we both frequented. He was a very outgoing young man with a winning personality and became very popular and much appreciated in our circle of friends. Later I heard that he and his wife separated and eventually were divorced.

A few years after Jim and I met, I accepted a teaching position in Midland and moved from Saginaw. Our paths no longer crossed so frequently and finally we totally lost track of one another. I taught in Midland for eighteen years before retiring in 1986 and then moved from Michigan to New Mexico in 1997. Jim and I had no contact with one another for over twenty years until that fateful day on the airplane at the Minneapolis-St. Paul Airport.

Our flight from Minnesota to Michigan was a delight for both of us. Jim and I quickly renewed our acquaintance and happily reminisced about all that had happened to the two of us during the intervening twenty plus years. I told him about what I had been doing since retirement and relived for him the story of my move to Albuquerque two years previously. He is years younger than I so he had trouble believing that I was returning to Michigan for my fiftieth year class reunion. Apparently his parents are roughly my age.

Jim told me his story too, and I found it much more fascinating than my mundane little tale. He related that since childhood he had felt that he was a female trapped in a male's body. No matter what activities in which he immersed himself, that specter remained with him constantly. Thinking that his unusual mindset might change if he were married, Jim proposed to a girl he had known since both were children. They married when they were still in their teens and began having children soon afterward. Though Jim was then a husband and a father, he still felt the same as he had previously. In his mind he was still a woman in the guise of a man. Marriage had not solved his problem; in fact it had exacerbated the situation because of the involvement of others.

Jim suffered in silence for several years in the untenable situation, not knowing which way to turn or what to do. At last he came to the conclusion that it was necessary for him to take positive action so he decided to reveal his secret to his wife. After Jim confessed his true feelings to her, the couple mutually agreed to separate and later went through a divorce. Fortunately they remained friends through it all. Jim began doing research on cross-gendered people and through his study realized that he was a prime candidate for a sex change. Over the course of the next few years he underwent all the mandatory psychological testing and accomplished the many necessary requirements for the alteration. Eventually the operations were performed successfully and Jim became Cheryl.

To me the transformation was nothing short of amazing. Previously Jim had been a handsome young man with blond to light red hair. His facial features were a bit delicate and his physical build was slight but those factors did not detract from his masculinity. He had what is usually called a swimmer's body—that is tall and slender. During the intervening years Jim had metamorphosed into a statuesque and beautiful woman. The one and only clue to his past sexual identity was his extreme height. Had I not recognized his face from his former persona, I would have had no clue that he wasn't born a female.

Once Cheryl became a woman in fact as well as emotionally, she felt more comfortable with herself and was then able to take up normal living once again. For several years while undergoing the change her life virtually had been put on hold. She returned to college and eventually earned a bachelor's degree in counseling and guidance. Cheryl said she had suffered untold psychological miseries during her earlier life and was proud of the fact that she had managed to overcome them. Therefore she felt a strong desire to help others who had various problems in order that they too could have the same successful experiences.

After graduation, Cheryl accepted a counseling position with a Denver, Colorado, clinic and had been employed there for a number of years prior to our reunion on the airplane in Minnesota. She is very fond of Denver and the liberal attitudes of its inhabitants. She loves the West and, like me, only returns to Michigan for occasional visits. Cheryl genuinely enjoys her work as a counselor because it provides her with a real sense of fulfillment.

When I questioned Cheryl about her reason for the trip to Michigan, I found her response to be intriguing. One of her sons, all of whom are now adults, was being married and of course had invited her to the nuptials. She accepted and was on her way to attend the ceremony. Though she was looking forward to seeing her children again; Cheryl confided in me that this was going to be the first time that she had appeared as a woman to certain members of her extended family. Understandably she was somewhat nervous concerning what their reactions might be. Cheryl indicated that experience had taught her that people often can accept something intellectually but when they actually see it in the flesh their reaction may be quite different. Upon hearing of her trepidation and anxiety, I assumed my school teacher façade and advised her to sail through the event with her head held high and to be proud of herself and all she had accomplished. In addition I told her to have a wonderful time at the wedding and let no small-minded bigots interfere with her enjoyment in any way. Hopefully she followed the advice and that all went well for her.

After the plane landed at MBS Airport near Saginaw, Cheryl and I became separated in the confusion of the arrival. Later I watched from across the baggage claim area as she was met by her son and several other family members—all of whom were equally as tall or even taller than she. Enthusiastically and warmly they greeted her with many hugs and kisses. It was most gratifying for me to see that she was fully accepted as an integral part of a caring and loving family. I felt certain that they would exert a strong force in supporting Cheryl during the coming family festivities which she was bravely facing, though with nervous trepidation

That particular visit to Michigan was a very good one. I enjoyed attending my fiftieth year high school class reunion and renewing acquaintances with my former classmates. During the past half century, time had wrought great changes in all of us. Many among us had become parents, grandparents and even great grandparents. The males in the group who still did have hair on their heads had seen it go from its original color to gray or white. I did note, however, that in one single aspect, very few of us had changed during the interim. Surprisingly what remained was the sound of our voices. If I closed my eyes and listened to the various people as they talked, I found that I could still picture them as they looked when we were still in high school some fifty years previously.

In all I spent about a week visiting relatives, looking up old friends and re-visiting many of my old haunts. I relished what turned out to be a nostalgic little tour through my past. However, having said that, I must confess that the one outstanding highlight of the entire trip was meeting Jim/Cheryl again and hearing his/her heartwarming story of sadness and despair turned into success, happiness and fulfillment. I felt very fortunate that I just happened to occupy the seat in the airplane right next to *the very tall lady*.

# CHAPTER 13
# UNFRIENDLY SAN FRANCISCO

I have often heard it said that of all the large American cities, San Francisco is the most similar to European cities. Supposedly it has its own individual character and ambiance that sets it far above other metropolitan areas such as Los Angeles, Chicago and Atlanta. The one and only time I visited "The City by the Sea", as San Francisco is called, I found it to be a real disappointment.

Just previous to visiting San Francisco I had spent a few days in Los Angeles and had a delightful time. The people were friendly and appeared to have a very welcoming attitude toward tourists spending time there. Everywhere I traveled on the crowded Los Angeles freeways the drivers were courteous to one another and

I had no difficulty driving anywhere I desired in the sprawling megalopolis.

From the City of Angels I took the coastal highway north through communities such as Oxnard, Ventura, Santa Barbara, Lompoc, and San Luis Obispo. Driving with the ocean waves crashing onto the rocks at my left and the splendid mountains rising on my right was exhilarating because the views were so spectacular. At the village of San Simeon, about one hundred fifty miles northwest of Los Angeles, I stopped to take a tour through the William Randolph Hearst Castle perched on a bluff overlooking the coastal village and the Pacific Ocean.

Though Mr. Hearst referred to his 270,000 acre complex simply as "the ranch," the main structure, the "ranch house", boasted 14 sitting rooms, 25 guest bedrooms and 41 bathrooms within its 73,500 square foot area. In addition to the main house there were three separate guest houses each containing four bedrooms with private bathrooms, and several additional sitting rooms. Two Olympic sized swimming pools provided recreation for Hearst's guests—one was indoors and the other was outside.

After admiring the conspicuous opulence of the castle, I drove back down the hill to the highway and continued toward my destination of San Francisco which lay about two hundred miles north along the coast. There had been recent television newscasts about wildfires raging in the Pacific highlands overlooking the city and, as I approached it I could see smoke billowing out from the tops of the Montera Mountains on my left. The gray smoke cast a pall over the lovely landscape and I probably should have taken that as an omen about unpleasant events to come.

My first stop in San Francisco was at the main Chamber of Commerce office in the downtown area. There I was shocked by the attitudes of the clerks on duty. They displayed no interest in tourists and gave me the distinct impression that their fine city was much too good to be sullied by riffraff wishing to visit it. I was able to learn little or nothing from them and became irritated as well as frustrated by the disdain they exhibited.

I soon left the office and went to seek a motel or hotel where I could rent a room for a few days while I took in what sightseeing possibilities there were. After several unsuccessful tries to locate a room in bed and breakfast establishments on Market Street, I finally found a vacancy in a quaint old hotel a few blocks north of there. Later I learned that it was in the tenderloin area, well-known for its high crime rate.

The hotel's quaintness was the only thing it had in its favor. The dark and gloomy lobby reminded me of something I might have seen in a horror movie. Its antiquated elevator, with an expandable metal grillwork for a door, wheezed and jerked its way unevenly to the third floor where my room was located. The small elevator car came to a noisy stop about a foot below the level of the floor so I was forced to hoist my luggage and step up to reach the hallway. The room, though large, was poorly lighted by one window which looked out upon an inadequate light shaft in the center of the building. The only view from the window was of the dirty brick wall on the opposite side of the shaft. Scratches, dings and marred surfaces on the mismatched furniture clearly indicated that it had suffered from many years of misuse. The door to the hallway showed hastily repaired patches designed to cover up the fact that the room had been violently broken into at some time or another.

The bathroom was in three parts. Separate doors hid the toilet and the shower which were both one step up from the floor of the room. The sink was in a dim corner and when I made the mistake of turning one of the taps, boiling water and steam gushed out. I tried to stem the flow by turning the faucet handle but to no avail so the room began filling with steam. Finally I discovered if I held the faucet handle down hard as I turned it toward the off position, the hot water stopped spewing forth. Thereafter the same thing happened each time I used the sink during my short stay at the hotel.

Because the hotel had no guest parking areas, the desk clerk directed me to a public parking garage two blocks away. Not only did the garage charge an exorbitant fee for daily and hourly parking, but the cavernous building contained many dark recesses where undesirable creatures lurked menacingly day and night. Each time I entered the structure I felt certain that I was risking my life to do so.

Driving a stick shift automobile in San Francisco is a harrowing experience. The city is built on forty-two steep hills. Most of the streets climb those hills and invariably at each cross street on the way up the precipitous slope, there is a stop sign. I found it nearly impossible to keep the car running with one foot on the brake and the other on the clutch. What I really needed was a third foot to use on the accelerator as well. More than once the engine stalled while I waited to proceed across the street and continue up the next block on the hill. My erratic driving and frequent stalls frustrated the local drivers (especially the women) who indicated their displeasure by honking loudly and punctuating their vituperation by giving me the finger as well. It came to seem as though that was the way San Franciscans waved a greeting to alien drivers in their midst.

The person or persons who told me that the best food in the entire world is served in San Francisco restaurants forgot to mention the fact that that same food is also probably the most expensive in the world. For dinner I purposely chose a restaurant that was not one of the better known ones. It was rather small and likely seated only about fifty or sixty patrons. After entering the restaurant, I was led to a table by the maitre d', who had his nose in the air and an expression on his face as if he smelled something revolting. When I was seated he disdainfully handed me the menu. My next clue that the prices were probably going to be extremely high was that the menu was nearly the size of the daily newspaper. I opened it to the first page and saw a list of some of the offerings. Rather than looking at the heading at the top of the page my eyes immediately scanned to the right side to check out the prices. Hmmm. They weren't nearly as high as I had anticipated. I noticed that I could actually afford most, but not all of the items listed. Then my eyes swept to the top of the page where I read, "APPETIZERS"! "These were the prices of the appetizers?" "Then how much would the regular entrees cost, for gosh sakes?" I turned the page and soon found out. I couldn't afford even the cheapest of them, let alone the most expensive. What to do? I simply didn't have enough chutzpah to walk out under the withering stare of the maitre d' who had seated me so I stayed. In a few minutes a waiter appeared and asked for my drink order. I chose coffee and he returned in a short while with it. Next he asked for my food order. I feigned a lack of hunger and limited my order to one of the less expensive appetizers that I had seen on the first page of the menu. Even so that still was the most expensive meal I had on the entire three week trip to California.

Some very wise person, I believe it was Mark Twain, once said, "The coldest winter I ever spent was a summer in San Francisco!" I would heartily agree with him. My trip to the city was during the middle of August when even frigid places like Alaska are warm, but not San Francisco. It was my assumption that sunny and warm California included all of the state but that was an error of gigantic proportions. While packing for the trip I included several pairs of walking shorts, many lightweight short-sleeved shirts and one very thin rain jacket—no long trousers, no sweaters and certainly no winter jacket. As it turned out the temperatures in the city never went above the mid fifties while I was there and that fact, plus the almost constant wind blowing off the Pacific, nearly convinced me that I would freeze to death before I quit the city's premises. I was even cold when the sun was directly overhead during the middle part of the day.

The one San Francisco sight that I definitely wanted to see was the Golden Gate Bridge which crosses the narrows between San Francisco Bay and the Pacific Ocean. It is one of the longest suspension bridges in the world. Warily I inched my way from the hilly downtown area to Highway 101 which, according to a sign, led toward the famous span. Eventually I arrived at the toll booth, paid the toll and drove over the mile-wide waterway which is called the Golden Gate. Like the rest of San Francisco, the bridge, too, was a keen disappointment. Frequent fogs shroud the bridge and on that particular morning it was especially thick and low lying. Only the lower portions of the bridge supports were visible through the pea soup-like mist. I was unable to see the majestic towers and miles of cable which support the floor of the bridge and give the gigantic structure its aesthetic and regal appearance. In a dejected funk, shortly after I had crossed the span, I located a place to turn around and, after once again paying the toll, re-crossed the bridge to San Francisco proper.

It is my distinct impression that the cable cars which ply their way up and down the precipitous streets were the only part of the city which lived up to their previous billing. They were quaint and exactly as I had envisioned they would be. I really enjoyed giving my car and my shattered nerves a rest by letting the cable cars make the stops at the cross streets instead of my being forced to do so with my stick shift auto. I observed no frustrated women drivers giving the cable car the finger gesture as they had done so frequently when I was at the wheel.

My original intention was to spend several days in San Francisco. I had planned to visit Fisherman's Wharf, Chinatown, Alcatraz Island, the Coit Memorial Tower atop Telegraph Hill, drive across the San Francisco – Oakland Bridge, and ride on the newly built BART (Bay Area Rapid Transport) subway system. However, twenty-four hours into the visit a combination of the weather, the city and its residents proved to be all I could tolerate. After spending a miserable night in the decrepit, but "quaint" hotel, I rescued my car from the formidable parking garage and pointed it out of San Francisco and toward Sacramento. That city is the capital of California and I found it much more to my liking.

People often wax eloquent in extolling the many perceived virtues of San Francisco. In fact, my encyclopedia opens the description of it in the following way: "San Francisco, California, the leading seaport of the Pacific Coast, is one of the world's most beautiful and unusual cities. Its mild climate, exciting scenery, fine restaurants, and unusual places to visit give the city a special charm. San Franciscans boast that every visitor ends up wanting to live there." I would be happy to inform those San Franciscans that I am one visitor to the city who, not only does not want to live there, but I don't even wish to visit it a second time. For me only twenty-fours in the snobbish, over rated place were more than adequate.

## CHAPTER 14
## TWO LOST DAYS IN PARIS

"I'm sorry monsieur, but due to security restrictions there are no longer any lockers for storing luggage in the Charles de Gaulle Airport." That statement from an information clerk sealed my fate for the day. Rather than spending a few pleasant hours in the center of Paris, as was my plan, I would be forced to remain with my luggage at the airport the entire day. Carrying two large suitcases plus a well-packed carry-on bag as I rode the train into the city and took part in a couple of walking tours would be an impossible task. Such had been my proposed itinerary for the day before I learned that I would be unable to check my luggage..

It was the middle of August, 2001, and I had just flown into Paris on a non-stop flight from Detroit. My arrival time was at 10:00 in the morning and late that afternoon I was to meet a couple of friends at the de Gaulle Airport which serves Paris and its suburbs. We planned to pick up a rental car there and spend a few days sightseeing along the route toward the village of Trigavu in Brittany where we had rented a house for two weeks. My friends were flying into Paris from London after spending a couple of weeks on the British Isles. Purposely, I had scheduled my arrival time about eight hours before their inbound flight. My last visit to Paris in 1953 was nearly fifty years ago and I wanted to use that free time to renew my acquaintance with the City of Light, as it is known throughout the world.

During the previous several weeks I had pored over tourist guide booklets about Paris and had decided on two walking tours that would allow me to see as much of the scenic city as was possible in a few short hours. The first of the tours in my grandiose plan would take me in a northwesterly direction from the commuter train station where I was to arrive, along the Right Bank of the Seine River past the Louvre Museum. It would continue along the Avenue des Champs Elysees to its end at the Arc de Triomphe. From the Arc I planned to walk south to the Eiffel Tower and finally follow the Left Bank of the Seine back to the Louvre once again. The second and much shorter proposed tour involved a walk from the Louvre along that same Left Bank in a southeasterly direction to the Ile de la Cite, the island in the Seine where the Cathedral of Notre Dame is located. I reasoned that those two walking tours, plus stopping at an outdoor café for lunch, would just about take up my free hours with enough time left over for returning to the airport and meeting my friends when they arrived at about 6:00 p.m.

The thought had never occurred to me that an international airport would have permanently done away with all of its luggage lockers. The dreary prospect of spending the next eight hours at the airport loomed before me. Despondently I searched for a luggage cart and after finding one, loaded my bags on it. Next I looked for a comfortable chair in which to sit. That task was much more daunting than locating a cart had been, because the airport was teeming with people arriving, departing or waiting for others who were doing so. Eventually I found a seat wedged in a small space between a pillar and a window. I pushed the cart toward it and sat down.

Fortunately I had an un-read book in my carry-on bag which I perused for a while. That soon proved to be unappealing so I decided to explore the terminal building. If it were not for pushing the luggage cart wherever I went, my exploration probably would have been much more interesting. My view from a central atrium showed a number of fascinating shops on several different levels. The problem was that the levels were separated by escalators. In order to go from floor to floor it would be necessary for me to unload the bags and then take the unlikely chance that there would be an available empty cart on the next floor. I chose to play it safe and remained on the same level where my friends' arrival gate was located.

During my wanderings I noticed a food service court and decided to have lunch. I reasoned that that activity would take up some of the slow-moving time stretching before me. However, it also presented yet another problem. There simply wasn't enough room to take the cart through the cafeteria line. So I had to abandon it outside the fenced in dining area. I nervously watched the cart while I waited in line and then hurriedly made my food selections. After that was done, fortunately I found a table immediately across the fence from the luggage cart.

Eating lunch only took up a half hour or so and there still remained about five hours before I would be meeting my friends. By that time the presence of the cart with my luggage was beginning to make me feel like a prisoner who was part of a chain gang. Everywhere I went it was a part of my entourage—even when I went to the bathroom!

I found another vacant seat and unenthusiastically went back to reading once again. Shortly thereafter an American couple approached the area where I was seated. They were in such close proximity to me that it was impossible for me not to overhear their strident conversation. The husband was abjectly apologetic and his wife was extremely angry. Apparently he was being forced to drop her off at the airport several hours before her airplane's scheduled departure because he had another commitment that required his presence. She was absolutely livid about having to wait there in the airport during the hours before her flight. After kissing her goodbye, the husband hurriedly made his exit. The still distraught lady threw herself into the seat next to me where she fumed silently.

I let her cool down for a little while before venturing to say anything. Then, tentatively, I mentioned having heard the exchange between the two of them and that I understood her plight and sympathized with her. That was all the encouragement she needed because immediately I was treated to a barrage of vicious complaints against her husband, the company he worked for, the airport, and life in general. After venting her anger and frustration, she seemed somewhat calmer and asked what had caused my wait in the airport. When she heard that tale of woe, the lady immediately became contrite and apologized for creating such a scene over a wait that wasn't even half as long as mine.

We introduced ourselves and I learned that her name was Adrienne. She and her husband, Donald, had been living in Paris for several years since his American company had transferred him there from New York City. At present Adrienne was on her way back to the United States to visit her family. By that time she seemed to be resigned to biding her time in the airport and her mood had improved considerably. Over the next three hours or so the two of us carried on a lively repartee as we compared notes about one another's life and circumstances. Apparently it really is true that "misery loves company" because our conversation helped to pass the seemingly unending time that both of us were forced to spend there.

Jerry R. Davis

When Adrienne's plane left the airport I was sorry to see her go but was encouraged by the knowledge that my friends' arrival time from London was less than an hour away. I spent that time devising a plan for seeing Paris on my way through after the two week stay in Brittany. For my return trip I had scheduled a flight out of Rennes, the only city in Brittany with a commercial airport. That flight would bring me back to Paris where I would board my transatlantic plane bound for the United States. Fortunately the only Paris Flight from Rennes was early in the morning and I would be arriving in Paris at about eight o'clock. Because my American flight didn't fly out until the middle of the afternoon, I reasoned that I could appear at the departure gate as soon as I arrived and check my luggage through to the United States. Then I would be free to take the interurban commuter train to the center of Paris and go on the walking tours that I had planned earlier. That seemed like a good plan and it made me feel somewhat mollified about the present unhappy situation.

My friends arrived on time; we located the rental car and then threaded our way through the horrendous Paris traffic toward the expressway. En route to the highway I did manage to glimpse the Eiffel Tower off in the distance to the south; therefore I was able to observe at least one of Paris's wonders. We headed out of the city on the A15 Expressway toward the northwest because we planned to spend the night in Giverny on the Epte River about forty miles from Paris. Giverny is site of the estate and gardens of Claude Monet, the world-renowned impressionist painter.

The next couple of weeks we occupied ourselves with seeing as many of the touristy sight-seeing locations as we could squeeze in. Not only did we visit Monet's home and gardens in Giverny, but also we saw the beautiful Gothic Amiens Cathedral, the ancient stone monoliths at Carnac, the Normandy beaches where the World War II D-Day invasion occurred, the lovely island abbey of Mont-St-Michel and many Medieval country chateaux as well. We gorged ourselves on the French cuisine and liberally sampled products of the local wineries. Contrary to the impression I had gained from my first visit there, we found the French people to be very warm and hospitable during our stay. They went out of their way to be friendly, helpful and courteous.

Trigavu, where our rental house was situated, was a small but picturesque old Brittany town with meandering streets lined with green hedges, a quaint business district, a beautiful slate-roofed church and delightful old stone houses. Our rental house was a four-hundred year old cut-stone structure with a red tiled roof, blue shutters and three foot thick walls. Inside were a living room, dining room, kitchen, five bedrooms and two baths. Both it and the attached owner's house next door were surrounded by a gated stone wall. The little compound contained an ancient stone workshop, a small fruit orchard, a vegetable and flower garden as well as a wooden chicken coop. The owner was gone for several days during our stay and she had encouraged us to gather the freshly laid eggs and use them for our breakfasts.

On the day I departed; my friends drove me to the Rennes Airport from Trigavu. I was somewhat saddened to be leaving the rural ambiance of the French countryside but equally eager to see the sights of Paris that I had missed at the start of the trip.

The Rennes Airport was a small one and the plane was a tiny jet with probably twenty passengers aboard. After an hour's flight we landed exactly on the dot of eight a.m. at de Gaulle and I picked up my luggage and headed for the Northwest/KLM desk to obtain a boarding pass and to check my luggage on through to Albuquerque, my eventual destination. I joined a short line and when it came my turn at the counter I presented my ticket and put my bags on the scale there. The attendant studied the ticket and then turned to me and said, "This flight doesn't leave until four p.m. this afternoon." "I know but I would like to check my luggage in now." was my reply. She said, "Oh I'm so sorry but we don't allow anyone to check in more than an hour to an hour and a half before departure time." "You mean that I can't do it now?" "That's right. If you return to this counter at two-thirty this afternoon, we will be happy to give you a boarding pass at that time and check your luggage through to your final destination." Curses! Foiled again!

Muttering unspeakable epithets to myself, I retrieved the bags from the scale and stalked across the terminal to a waiting luggage cart and loaded them on. I simply couldn't believe that this was happening to me all over again! Once more I was going to be "chained" to a luggage cart for nearly an entire day at the airport!

What a dreary prospect! What miserable luck! The more I thought about the next six or eight hours of utter boredom within those uninspiring walls, the worse my gloom became.

The short glimpse of the Eiffel Tower I had had from the window of the rental car on our way out of the city two weeks prior to that, was my one and only view of any of Paris's sightseeing possibilities on that trip. I had visited and enjoyed many sights that rural France had to offer the tourist but, other than the tower, I saw none of those in Paris.

Eventually the long and tedious hours of the day wound their slow way down and I finally was able to board the airplane. We took off on time and I slept during most of the seven hour flight to Detroit. After a short layover there I caught my connecting flight and at about ten-thirty in the evening landed in Albuquerque where I was met by a friend.

At home I fell into bed and into a deep and dreamless sleep. The next morning was September 11, 2001. I slept late and awoke to the news on television that terrorists had flown planes into the twin towers of the World Trade Center in New York City as well as into the Pentagon Building in Washington, D.C. Ironically I had been through part of that same air space only twelve hours previously and that to me was a little too close for comfort.

The friends with whom I had stayed in the rental house in France were scheduled to fly out a few days after I did. I later learned that all their return flights to the United States were cancelled and they had to stay in Europe for several additional days until the normal transatlantic schedules resumed once again. Only then were they able to re-book their flights for the return trip.

I count myself extremely fortunate that I arrived home on time and safely when I consider the five thousand people who lost their lives, the additional thousands who were injured and the tens of thousands of travelers who were seriously inconvenienced as a result of the terrorist attacks. When compared to all of that my two "lost" days in the de Gaulle Airport are a mere nothing.

# CHAPTER 15
# TRAVELING SICK, BUT NOT
# SICK OF TRAVELING

"Daddy, Daddy, please stop the car. I have to throw up!" shouted the seven year old boy from the crowded depths of the vehicle's rear seat. That was my first real experience of being sick while on the road, but it was destined to be repeated many times before a solution was found.

Being ill is never fun, but being ill while traveling in foreign locations is especially disconcerting. I am the type of person who prefers to be in the safe haven of his own home when he is sick. The fact remains, however, that anyone who does much traveling is eventually going to have the experience of being ill while far away from his familiar environs. I am no exception to that rule and have experienced a number of occasions where I was under the weather while on the move.

From the time I was a small child until the present I have been afflicted with motion sickness while riding in the rear seat of most automobiles. One of my family's favorite entertainments during my childhood was to go on Sunday drives. Gasoline prices were low at the time and all of us enjoyed that inexpensive way of seeing parts of the country that we hadn't previously experienced. Initially, Mother and Dad sat in the front seat and my three siblings and I occupied the rear seat. Those expeditions became a misery for me as I would become nauseous before we had gone more than a few miles and would remain so until we returned home. My dad repeatedly told me to only look at those items off in the distance and not those near to the car. He felt that perhaps the rapid movement past roadside trees, fence posts, bushes, etc. was causing my nausea. My attempts to follow his directions proved futile as, invariably, I still would become ill. How or when we learned that if I sat in the front seat I felt no motion sickness, I don't recall, but we did and from that point on I occupied a place between Mother and Dad in the front. From that vantage point I was able to enjoy the sights on all the drives without constantly feeling as though I had to upchuck.

My first bad experience with sea sickness was aboard the *Karlstad*, a small Swedish ship. That occurred as we were crossing the Atlantic Ocean on my first trip to Europe in 1953. Shortly after we boarded at Montreal, Canada, and steamed from the St.

Lawrence Seaway into the Atlantic, my stomach began to feel queasy. I became sick enough that I went to my cabin and spent the entire first day and night of the ten-day crossing lying in my bunk. If I so much as lifted my head off the mattress I immediately was overcome with nausea.

That first night especially seemed interminable to me. My cabin and bunk were situated crosswise of the ship, and as I lay there the bed rocked from end to end. First my head was up and my feet were down and then my feet were up and my head was down. To add to my mental torment, the ship, as it rocked from side to side, often seemed as though it would not be able to right itself again. I had visions of the vessel falling over on its side and all of us plunging into the ocean depths. Finally, toward morning I fell into a fitful sleep.

When I awoke the seas were calmer and so was my stomach. In fact my nausea had left me entirely and consequently I was ravenous for something to eat. I ate a large breakfast and kept it down with no difficulty. In direct contrast to the first, the next nine days on the ship were delightful. Though we sailed through some fairly rough seas at times, I experienced no further vestiges of sea sickness. Apparently I had earned my "sea legs," for that particular cruise, with my twenty-four bout with the malady.

My next experience with sea sickness occurred in November of that same year as I was returning from Europe on the huge ocean liner, *The Queen Elizabeth*. We boarded the ship at the French seaport of Le Havre on the southern coast of the English Channel. From there we sailed west between England and France and entered the Atlantic Ocean. Since I had been through my sea sickness "trial by fire" aboard the *Karlstad* on the way to Europe about six months earlier, I assumed that it wouldn't trouble me on this second voyage. That assumption was totally incorrect!

The smaller ship, the *Karlstad,* met the seas with a smooth side to side movement, but the much larger, *Queen Elizabeth's* lateral movements were jerky. It seemed to shudder over and over again as we made our way through the waves. My stomach rebelled and once again, before we were more than a few hours from port, I became queasy and had to take to my bed. For me sea sickness never seems to last more than one day's duration; because by the second day I was up and about and feeling fine. The next five days of the six-day sailing were very pleasant and I experienced no more nausea.

Since those two experiences in 1953, I have sailed on quite a number of cruise ships—through the Great Lakes, along the length of Puget Sound to Canada, across the North Sea from England to Belgium and in the Caribbean Sea. Only once during the intervening fifty years has sea sickness again had its way with me. In January, 2003, I went on a week's cruise aboard the *Norwegian Dawn.* I boarded the vessel at Miami, Florida, and from there we sailed to two locations on Mexico's Yucatan Peninsula, then north to Key West, Florida, and east to the Bahaman Islands before returning to Miami. One of the two ports of call in Mexico was at Cozumel

Island. There the harbor was too shallow for a ship as large as the *Dawn,* so it dropped anchor a mile or so from shore and we were picked up by small ferry boats and taken to the pier.

During that half hour trip we experienced extremely rough sailing. High waves pounded the small boat and it rocked from side to side. The cabin floor tilted back and forth at what seemed like forty-five degree angles. I even began to lose my sense of what direction was up and what direction was down. About ten minutes into the trip I knew that I had to get to a bathroom because I was about to lose my breakfast. I got up from the bench where I had been sitting and aimed myself toward the stern where the restrooms were. Walking was nearly impossible and I staggered from post to post across the heaving floor. The thirty foot trek seemed to take forever. Finally I made it to the restroom door and lurched through. I fell to my knees in front of the toilet and threw up everything that was in my stomach.

Eventually I managed to find my way back to the bench where I had been sitting. One of my cruise companions mentioned that he had never seen anyone turn quite as green as I had before I left for the restroom. By that time we were approaching the docking place at the pier and the calmer water there allowed the ferryboat to become relatively stable. We disembarked, did a few hours of sightseeing on Cozumel Island, and then returned to the ferry later that afternoon. Thankfully, the return trip to the *Dawn* was much smoother than the first.

159

On my first visit to Mammoth Cave National Park in central Kentucky, I experienced a painful episode of violent illness. My traveling companion, Steve, and I drove from Michigan to the park in two days. We stopped for the night at a motel along the highway near Indianapolis, Indiana, and then arrived at the cavern about noon the next day. That afternoon and the following day were spent going on several of the underground tours and frequenting the museum and gift shop at the visitor's center on the surface.

Up until then I felt fine but that night things began to change. I went to bed in the motel room we had rented and almost immediately dropped off to sleep. In a short time I was awakened by a sharp pain in my stomach area. One of the recurring problems during much of my life is that my body produces kidney stones. The pain, I concluded, must be another attack of that sort.

Previously I had learned that the only time kidney stones cause serious pain is during their movement from the kidney through the ureter to the bladder. The ureter is a long, narrow tube and as the stone, which is very rough textured, is forced through that tube it tears at the walls thus causing excruciating pain, sometimes for hours on end. Also I had learned that if I could bear the agony for the period of time of the stone's passage to the bladder, then the pain would cease immediately. Therefore, I decided to tough it out and wait for nature to take its course.

That entire night was a miserable one because the hours passed agonizingly slowly. When morning finally arrived the pain had abated somewhat but was far from completely gone. We got up and went to a restaurant for breakfast. I wasn't able to eat anything but dry toast soaked in weak coffee. Our plan for that day had been to visit another natural cavern near where Mammoth Cave is located. Steve asked me if I were up to it. I decided that since that cave was one we could view while driving through it, perhaps I could tolerate the visit. During the tour the pain returned with a real vengeance and I knew that I had to do something about it. After conferring, we decided to head directly back home to Michigan. Steve drove the entire five hundred miles only stopping for gas when necessary and we arrived back in Saginaw late in the evening.

Still convinced that I was having a kidney stone attack, I immediately went to bed. However, no matter how many blankets I piled on, I could not get warm. My teeth chattered and I felt as if I were freezing. An hour or so of that agony convinced me that something other than kidney stones was affecting me and I went to the emergency room of one of the local hospitals.

The emergency room doctor who examined me said that it wasn't a kidney stone attack but instead was much more serious. It was a case of appendicitis. In fact, he added, my appendix was ready to burst. He phoned a surgeon who told him to prepare me for an emergency operation and that he would be there in minutes. When the surgeon arrived it was determined that no operation could take place until they were able to get my body temperature down.

The reason for the chills I had experienced at home was that an extremely high fever was raging through my body.

The doctor's method for reducing the fever seemed like a medieval torture to me. They wrapped me in a sheet and covered me with ice! Though very painful, the method worked and my temperature went down. However, before they could get me into the operating room and properly prepped, the raging fever returned. So, once again, I was packed in ice. Then the doctor successfully performed the appendectomy. He told me later that my appendix was in worse condition than any he had seen previously. He was amazed that it had not burst before he was able to remove it.

In the spring of 1996 I traveled to Hong Kong to visit my nephew, Daniel, and his wife, Jennifer, who were living and working there. I had purchased my airplane tickets months before the departure date. A little over a week prior to the day the trip was to begin, I suffered a kidney stone attack. Because the trip was imminent, I called the urologist for an appointment. After explaining to the doctor about my proposed trip to the Orient, he indicated that we should do something about the stone immediately rather than taking the chance that it would flare up again while I was in Asia. Under normal conditions he would have waited for the stone to descend to the bladder of its own volition, but in this case he felt that waiting would be a mistake which could have serious consequences. Therefore he scheduled me for an operation the next day during which he would zap the kidney stone with a laser beam. The laser would break the stone into tiny bits which then could easily traverse the ureter to the bladder.

The operation went well and in a day or so I was up and about and seemed to be recovering nicely. The next day when I was eating with some friends at a restaurant, I began to have a definite feeling of "fullness" in my bladder area and I was unable to urinate. The pressure grew and grew until I returned to the urologist's office, with no appointment. He saw me immediately and realized that I was in misery and then catheterized me to relieve the pressure.

Because the Hong Kong trip was looming ever nearer—only a day or two from then—I asked the doctor what I should do if that occurred while I was abroad. He suggested that I purchase a catheter kit at a pharmacy and take it with me on the trip. I did so but fortunately never had to use it.

Though I didn't have any further problem with kidney stones on that trip to the Orient, I did, however, contract a case of "Montezuma's Revenge." Montezuma's Revenge is a stomach disorder that many tourists incur when they travel in Latin American countries, such as Mexico, thus the name. The local water supply and the foods apparently aren't treated in the same way that American water and foods are, therefore, they may cause intestinal havoc. By that time I had been to Mexico three times and had experienced no stomach problems, therefore I felt that I was immune to the illness. In addition to that I had never heard of the "Revenge" attacking travelers in the Far East so I didn't give it a thought. That was a foolish error on my part.

The first two days of my stay I felt fine, but on the third day it struck. My nephew, Daniel, and I had called for a taxi to take us from Hong Kong Island over to Kowloon Peninsula where we were planning to visit the newly completed Mormon Temple (non-Mormons are allowed to visit the temples before they are dedicated). The taxi arrived at the apartment complex, we boarded it and before we had gone a mile, I had to ask the driver to stop because I had to throw up. I did so along the side of the road. After that I felt better so we continued on our way. We arrived at the temple and had our tour but hadn't left the building before the second attack hit me. I asked the guide if there were a bathroom available. He was unused to a toilet being referred to as a "bathroom" and asked me if I desired to take a bath. I said, "No, but I do have to vomit immediately!" My panic apparently got through to him at that point and he directed me to the men's toilet where I threw up once again.

During our return taxi trip to the apartment the driver had to stop two additional times for me. By the time we arrived I was exhausted from retching and from the dry heaves that followed immediately after. At the apartment I went to bed and stayed there for the next twenty-four hours only getting up for quick trips to the bathroom for more of the same. Daniel prepared some hot, clear broth for me to sip and finally I was able to keep that down by the end of the following day. The next morning I was somewhat weak, but otherwise feeling fine and I had no recurrence of the problem during the balance of my two week stay in Hong Kong.

Over the past fifty years I have traveled many thousands of miles and have seen literally hundreds of different places of interest. During the vast majority of those trips I have felt perfectly healthy and suffered no vestiges of any type of sickness. The few cases of illness while traveling that I have cited above do not in any way detract from the joy I experience in visiting "Far away places with strange sounding names" (as the well-known song puts it). After all those years have elapsed I still experience great excitement in boarding some type of vehicle, be it automobile, train, airplane or ship, for parts unknown because I know that there always will be many things of interest to enjoy along the route as well as at the end of the trip.

# CHAPTER 16
# A SCENIC MOUNTAIN TRAIN RIDE

"I was torn between watching the passing scenes and watching the scenes of the passengers." That was a quote from an article that I wrote for the newsletter of an Albuquerque organization, called Prime Timers New Mexico, to which I belong. In the article I was describing a wine tasting event in which I participated aboard a narrow gauge railroad in southwestern Colorado during the early fall of 2003. The scenes I observed while on the train trip were of two contrasting types. The first type was the majestic natural beauty of Colorado's San Juan Mountains on the fifty mile roundtrip and the second type was made up of the many humorous examples of drunken revelry inherent in an event where alcohol flows very freely and in great quantities.

We began the train trip in Durango, Colorado, a colorful and lovingly restored former mining town of approximately 15,000 residents that contains hundreds of handsome Victorian homes and business places. The imposing pink and white four-story Strater Hotel was built in 1889 after a disastrous fire destroyed much of the town and it now dominates Main Street at the center of the business district. Like many of the historic old homes and other business buildings, the hotel has been fully restored to its original Nineteenth Century grandeur, both inside and out, and richly deserves its place as the hub of the now thriving tourist town. As one walks along the tree-shaded streets of Durango, it is easy to ignore the crowds of tourists and imagine that you have been transported back one hundred and twenty-five years in history to the storied mining era of that part of the Colorado Rockies.

The Durango and Silverton Narrow Gauge Railroad, on which we were to ride, was originally built in 1881 to link the gold and silver mining areas of the San Juan Mountains to the ore processing plants and smelters situated in other areas of Colorado. The railroad thrived in that capacity for approximately fifty years and hauled thousands of tons of ore during that period of time. Eventually the veins of ore became depleted and the line was used less and less. As that occurred, forward-looking entrepreneurs changed the railroad's main purpose from that of ore hauler to transporter of sightseers.

The mountainous countryside through which the train travels is breathtaking in its beauty and now attracts over 200,000 tourists to the area annually. The narrow gauge railroad today is the main tourist draw of the entire area and those visitors are the region's major source of income.

At about eleven a.m. we boarded the train behind the quaint, stick style Victorian railroad station on the southern edge of Durango. As we left the station for the train platform and presented our tickets to the attendant, each of us was given a stemmed wine glass. Most of those glasses were well broken in to their intended purpose by the time of our return late that afternoon. The three hundred plus participants sought seats either in the enclosed yellow painted cars or located standing room in the open-air observation cars. Those observation cars were roofed but had no sides and, they too, were a bright yellow in color. The cars presented a vivid contrast to the enormous, noisy, black steam engine which pulled the train.

In general most of the passengers seemed quiet, dignified and cheerful and there was little noise that could not be explained by the fact that there was a large number people boarding the train and attempting to locate individual places for enjoying the scenic excursion ahead.

At last the engine's whistle blew and a few minutes later the train lurched into motion. The speed was kept very low as we passed through the length of Durango heading for the mountains that bordered it on the north. We crossed traffic-crowded streets and pedestrian-filled sidewalks between the lowered wooden protective gates. The clanging of the crossing bells provided musical accompaniment for the train's whistle as we inched our way through the crowded and scenic town.

No wine was poured until we had left the city limits of Durango behind and had begun the assent into the mountain heights that brushed the city's northern edge. The reason for non-imbibing on the train while it was in the town limits was never explained to us but I would assume that it had to do with the liquor and alcohol consumption laws of the area. However, as soon as we had passed the town's boundary, people immediately headed for the observation cars where the wine stewards began popping corks and dispensing the many different varieties of wines to all who desired them. Wine has never been my drink of choice, so I had previously decided that on the excursion I would content myself with sipping soda pop or mineral water and nibble at the hors d'oeuvres which were in plentiful supply. I planned to leave the hard drinking to others. That self proclaimed limitation turned out to be a fortunate choice because, as the trip progressed, I found that my entertainment was of a two-fold nature. Not only did I enjoy the precipitous and forest-covered mountainous scenery surrounding us, but in addition. I was thoroughly amused by observing the hilarious antics of those passengers who liberally imbibed the proffered spirits.

Beyond Durango the train track followed along the Animas River and it made its way in a generally northeastern direction. Our destination for the excursion was a stop called Cascade Canyon which is situated about halfway between Durango and the little town of Silverton. It lies approximately twenty five miles from each of the mountain settlements.. The canyon is roughly four thousand feet higher in elevation than Durango, consequently the train was climbing constantly to get there. I could hear the labored chugging of the train's engine as it made its way up the steep route. The railroad bed had been scratched out of the side of the mountain with little room to spare and it contained a large number of switchbacks. Many times when I looked out the window I could see the engine and the forward cars above and to our left as we snaked our sinuous way up the mountainsides. At other times the passengers on the left side of the cars could actually touch the craggy sides of the gouged-out mountain through the open windows; whereas the passengers on the opposite side could look nearly straight down two hundred feet or more to the Animas River flowing along the valley at the base of the mountain.

It was late in September and the fall coloration was just beginning to appear. Though the color change was in its early stages, we still were able to see some beautiful and dramatic contrasts between the bright yellows of the aspen foliage and the deep, dark green of the pine and fir trees. Adding to those hues were occasional groves of cottonwoods which lined the sides of the river and contributed their own singular gold pigments to the varied autumn palette. The scenery was rich with vibrant color.

Before we were even an hour into the trip, it became obvious to me that the alcohol was having two main effects on those who were drinking it. The first effect I noted was that their balance began to fail. A narrow gauge train while traveling across mountainous terrain, tends to jerk from side to side and from front to back making walking very difficult even for sober travelers. Early in the trip the passengers had carefully made their way up and down the aisles grasping the seat backs to steady themselves along the way.

However, once those same passengers had drunk enough wine, they often lurched all over the aisles and even occasionally landed in one another's laps as they made their halting way through the cars. Those who chose to wear light colored tops or shirts soon found them spotted here and there with a variety of slopped wines of different colors. But no one seemed very perturbed by the resulting dishabille. In fact, I heard one passerby point out several wet stains on the blouse of a girl whom he was standing near. Her reply was that she was proud of them and thought of them as badges of honor that added to the ambience of the wine tasting trip.

A few of the really inebriated passengers seemed in dire peril of falling from the train as they unsteadily moved from one lurching car to another. The narrow, shifting open platforms connecting the various cars were difficult to cross in the best of times and were even more treacherous when the person doing the crossing was somewhat shaky. One careless misstep and he or she could be sent hurling down the side of the mountain to the river below. The railroad bed was extremely narrow because it had been scooped out of the rocky mountainside and had no room to spare. It was nearly against the craggy rock wall on one side and next to a precipitous drop-off on the other.

The second effect that the alcohol had on the imbibers was that it seemed to lessen their hearing ability drastically. In order for the drinkers to make their companions comprehend what they were saying it was necessary for them to shout. Consequently the overall noise level on the train began to escalate dramatically. In fact, the once staid, dignified and relatively quiet passengers had evolved into a screeching mob of reveling party animals. Sadly the vast majority of them seemed completely oblivious to nature's colorful artistry as we steamed through the spectacular autumn scenery.

After a two and a half hour ride in a generally northeasterly direction from Durango, the train backed into a siding at our destination, Cascade Canyon. There, in a lovely valley next to the east bank of the Animas River, we were to have lunch, provided by the railroad, under the roof of a large covered pavilion. I observed that though the train had stopped moving and the passengers had descended to the ground, not all the lurching ceased. One young lady in particular seemed to have a problem with her balance as she unceremoniously fell to the ground when she attempted to walk between the stopped train and the place where lunch was being served. The girl's noisy companions merely dragged her along the ground until she was able to gain her footing once again. Obviously she was feeling no pain whatsoever.

After lunch a few of us took a leisurely walk through the forested area that lined both sides of the stream and admired the beauty of the rock-strewn rapids as the fast moving water flowed downriver. About a quarter of a mile upstream there was a pedestrian suspension bridge from which we were provided with spectacular views of the river as it meandered it way through the trees. From one angle on the bridge I could even see a snow-covered mountain peak far off to the northeast. It foretold the cold winter which would soon engulf that part of Colorado.

At about the middle of the afternoon, the engineer sounded the train's whistle warning us to board and head once again for Durango. The entire atmosphere of the return trip was quite different from the outbound one. Apparently the combination of alcohol and full stomachs caused most of the revelers to become lethargic so the noise level was much more subdued. While I sauntered from car to car, I noticed sleeping passengers all along the way. Once again only a small handful of them observed the natural wonders that the train passed en route.

A change in the weather caused the two hour return trip to Durango to be very different from the earlier one, though equally impressive. By that time the skies had filled with low lying steel-gray clouds and a light rain had begun to fall. The dark, tree-covered mountain slopes took on an almost sinister quality. They seemed to hulk menacingly over the train as it snaked its way carefully down the switchbacks along their rocky sides. About halfway to our destination we crossed a precipitous trestle bridge that took us from one side of the Animas River Gorge to the other. From high above we could see the rushing river as it poured through the narrow gap below.

The route led past two placid-looking mountain lakes nestled in deep valleys between the slopes. Their waters appeared to be totally unspoiled and natural because, other than the train tracks, I could see no signs of human activity in the surrounding area. It appeared to be a virtual mountain Shangri-la where man had not as yet left his distinctive and often ugly mark.

Late in the afternoon, just as dusk began to envelope the landscape we pulled into Durango once again. The scenic mountain train ride ended where it had begun that morning, at the restored Victorian train station on the southern edge of town. The sleeping passengers roused themselves, left the train quietly and headed sedately to the parking lot where they had left their vehicles. Since late that morning the travelers had metamorphosed from quiet and dignified early on to boisterous and loud later in the day and finally ended the trip subdued and in an apparently somber frame of mine.

All my life I have been a "people watcher' and, in addition to that, I have always appreciated natural beauty. I love to observe humans in a variety of situations in order to see how they act or react to what they encounter. But, equally as much, I enjoy observing nature and all its marvels. That wine tasting train trip in southwestern Colorado gave me a two-fold opportunity for experiencing both of those passions.

# CHAPTER 17
# THE FINAL VISIT

The last time I saw my father when he was still alive was in August of 2001. Each year, after I moved from Michigan to New Mexico, I would make a trip east to see relatives and friends and to renew my acquaintance with all the familiar places where I had spent the major portion of my life. The annual junket was something I looked forward to with anticipation. I really enjoyed seeing the people I had taught with at Central Intermediate School in Midland, the people with whom I had volunteered at the Mid Michigan Regional Medical Center as well as the many relatives and the friends from my childhood who still lived in the Thumb Area of the state. The few days in Michigan always sped by because, invariably, there were more people to visit than there was time to do the visiting. However, one part of the annual trip I did not look forward to—in fact I dreaded it. That was when I went to the Gladwin Pines Nursing Home to see my father. Dad had suffered a massive stroke in January of 1997 and had been living there in a totally helpless state during the past four years.

Of course I didn't know then that it would be my last visit with Dad, but I strongly suspected so. My brother, who had been to see him earlier in the summer, warned me that he had failed terribly since we both had seen him the previous year. Therefore, I was facing the visit with even more reluctance than usual. Dad and his deplorable state were on my mind as I boarded the airplane in Albuquerque and also during much of the flight from there to Minneapolis, Minnesota, where I would change planes for the last leg of the trip to Michigan. Unpleasant and troubled thoughts constantly surged through my mind about the background events that had brought Dad to his present condition.

I recalled how active he had been after he retired at the age of sixty-five. For the next twenty-four years he always planted and cared for an enormous garden, he tended his lawn, did all his own maintenance on the house and even put a new roof on it when he was in his early eighties. He took good care of my mother during her last years before her death in 1995. Because she, for the most part was unable to do so, Dad did practically all the housework. He made the beds, cleaned the bathroom and the kitchen, washed the dishes, dusted the furniture, went grocery shopping, vacuumed the carpets and even helped Mother with much of the meal preparation.

I remembered how lonely Dad was after Mother died. They had been married sixty-six years by that time and though they often disagreed with one another, nonetheless they were a solid team. When Mother passed away, the team that had seemed so permanent was instantaneously dissolved. For months Dad felt completely at loose ends and could find little or no purpose in life. Time dragged by for him and he lost much of his zest for living.

Then I recalled how the solution to Dad's lonely condition came in the form of a neighbor lady. Her name was Irene Gould and she was a widow who lived around the corner from him. She and her husband had been friends with both Mother and Dad ever since they had moved into the area about ten years prior to that. Irene's husband died a few years before Mother, so she had been experiencing the loneliness of single living for some time already. Irene and Dad began going places and doing things together and the relationship provided what both of them had been needing—companionship.

Dad's outlook on living began to change immediately. He once again seemed to have a purpose in life and smiled and laughed much more easily. Dad was about two years younger than Irene, who was ninety years old at the time, and he gracefully accepted the good natured teasing he got from my relatives and me about dating an "older lady." Frequently we would meet to go out for lunch or dinner together and all of us thoroughly enjoyed one another's company. Never did I get the impression that Irene was in any way attempting to take the place of our mother, but invariably she was kind, considerate and loving to all of us—especially to Dad. She effortlessly fit into the family circle and my siblings and I were grateful that the two of them had found one another and were so happy together.

I remembered how physically and mentally active Dad remained, in spite of his advanced age. That winter one of the volunteer tasks he assigned himself was to use his snow-blower to clear out the driveways of his neighbors, including Irene's. In addition he read voraciously and kept excellent records of his income, expenditures, contributions, et cetera for the accountant who computed his yearly taxes. Upon occasion he and Irene drove the thirty-five miles to Midland where I lived and we three would go on outings together. Sometimes we visited relatives in the vicinity or went even further afield and attended local celebrations in the Vassar area of Michigan's Thumb. That was where Dad and Mother had lived for most of their married years. Dad and Irene's time together seemed idyllic and golden, but that was soon to change dramatically.

As the airplane winged its way toward Minnesota, the memory of the frantic telephone call from my sister replayed itself. Joanne told me that Dad had had a massive stroke and was in the emergency room of the Gladwin Hospital. Immediately I put aside what I was doing and hurriedly drove to the hospital. There I found Dad in an ER cubicle surrounded by nursing personnel. His face had a twisted look because one side of his mouth drooped downward. He was unable to speak but he did seem to understand what was being said to him. No matter how hard he struggled to do so he could not respond to questions with words or sentences. Instead he was forced to use nods or head shakings to get his points across. He was unable to move the fingers on one of his hands or the arm itself, so it hung uselessly at his side.

For the first time in my entire life, I saw real terror reflected in Dad's eyes. From my perspective he always had been completely fearless no matter what known or imagined peril faced him. I found it most disconcerting to see him in such a helpless and frightened state of mind. My sister and I felt equally as helpless as he because we were able to do nothing for him. We were forced to content ourselves with merely letting him know that we were there for him and would provide support in any way we could.

Later, after piecing the story together from different sources, we learned that Dad had gotten up at his usual time that morning and had prepared and eaten his breakfast as was his normal pattern. Since it had snowed the night previously, he took his snow-blower out of the garage and cleared the night's accumulation from his driveway and sidewalk. Then he went over to Irene's house and did the same for her. The two of them had coffee together and chatted for a few minutes before he returned home. During their conversation Dad told Irene that he had to take care of some business at the bank. After putting the snow-blower back in the garage, he backed his car out and drove across town to the Chemical Bank on Cedar Street. He parked his car on the side street next to the bank building and went inside. He walked up to a teller's window and asked a question about one of his savings accounts. The teller turned away from him to look up the needed information on the computer and, after she located it, turned back to Dad. But he was no longer standing at the window! In that brief time he had had the stroke and was lying helplessly on the floor. He was unable to rise. In fact, though Dad lived for over five years beyond that point, he never stood on his own again. A bank employee telephoned the paramedics who arrived shortly and he was whisked off to the hospital in an ambulance.

I thought about what a doleful sight it was to observe Dad during the next couple of weeks as he lay helplessly in his hospital bed. He struggled in vain to make intelligible sentences. Though he could say a few words, it was impossible for him to string them together into anything logical that could be understood by others. Any time he left his room it was necessary for him to be lifted out of bed to a wheel chair. Because the stroke had affected his throat muscles making swallowing difficult, all his food had to be the consistency of pureed baby food. Even his liquids like milk and water had to be of that same consistency. He was unable to use the bed pan or the bed urinal so he was catheterized and diapered. I soon noticed that being incontinent was the aspect of his illness that bothered him more than any other part. He was always a very proud and independent man and found it most demeaning to rely on hospital help for taking care of all his very basic and personal needs.

Dad's doctor informed my sister and me that, considering his condition, home care would be nearly impossible as well as being prohibitively expensive. He strongly recommended that we make application to have Dad enter a residence facility that provided total nursing care for its patients. We inquired about the Gladwin Pines Nursing Home attached to the hospital, but learned that it had no openings at that time. Eventually we were able to place him in a similar facility at Roscommon, about fifty miles north of Gladwin. Though the nursing home was a good one, we felt that it was unsatisfactory because of the distances we had to travel to visit with Dad. I had to drive eighty-five miles each way and Joanne had to travel about sixty miles each way. However, it could serve as a stop-gap solution until an opening occurred at the home in Gladwin. Fortunately, after he spent a month in Roscommon, we were able to have Dad moved to Gladwin where he had lived for the past four and a half years. During that time Dad was unable to say many words, but one thing he made abundantly clear—he wanted to die because he found his existence intolerable.

At that point my thoughts about Dad were interrupted by the flight attendant announcing that we were approaching the Minneapolis – St. Paul Airport. I was soon occupied with stowing my carry on bag and getting ready for the landing. After we touched down and had taxied to the gate, we exited the airplane and I went into the terminal to find the gate for my connecting flight to Michigan. As was usually the case it was located in another concourse and far from our arrival gate so I made the lengthy trek across the huge airport. En route I stopped to have lunch in the food commons and then arrived at the correct gate with time to spare before my flight's departure.

When I was once again airborne and settled into the second flight my thoughts automatically returned to Dad. I pondered the extreme differences between his past life and the present sorry state of his existence. His total helplessness in that situation contrasted dramatically with the life he had known previously. During his long tenure on earth he always had been an active, healthy and robust man. He went to bed early, slept the deep sleep of someone who had toiled hard physically, and rose early each morning to meet the challenges of the new day.

Dad grew up on a small Mid-western farm in the Thumb area of Michigan's Lower Peninsula. Each member of the family was required to share the burden of work the enterprise entailed. In spite of the family's strenuous efforts, the farm was not a very productive one and even in the best of times it provided only a marginal living for the two adults and eight children who lived there.

Like his father before him, Dad chose agriculture for his career. Prior to purchasing his first farm he had worked for a few years at the Chevrolet Assembly Plant in Flint, about thirty miles from his home. Shortly after he and Mother married in 1929 they put a small down payment on an eighty acre farm a few miles from his parent's home. In order to subsidize the farm and make the yearly loan payments on it, he continued to work at the Chevrolet factory. Every waking moment that Dad was at home he labored in the fields and farmyard. During the spring, summer and fall he tilled the soil and cultivated the crops in the fields. In winter he worked equally as hard caring for the dairy herd he had established in addition to tending to the flock of chickens and the few hogs that he raised for slaughter. Dad's endeavors, though personally gratifying, were nonetheless physically exhausting.

I recalled how Dad's labors eventually began to pay off. He sold the first farm and we moved to a much larger one near Vassar, about five miles away. By that time he had left the factory job because he no longer had to supplement the farm earnings with a second income. However, the new acreage, which was over three times the size of the original, required even more physical labor so the day in and day out toil increased proportionally. For the next twenty-five years he happily worked in his rural paradise. Dad loved all living things, both plant and animal, and he relished the wide variety of activities connected with running a farm. His chosen career occupied him totally and required his complete concentration. He was rarely under the weather and took no vacations during those years.

As Dad approached his mid-fifties, he realized that it would be necessary for him to make some changes in his lifestyle. By that time all of my siblings and I had left the farm for other occupations and therefore he was forced to run the large enterprise alone.

185

Though he still thoroughly loved his farm and the life it provided, he knew that he could no longer manage it by himself. Dad made the painful decision to sell the farm. He couldn't bear to get rid of all of it so he kept three acres just north of the old farmhouse and on that plot he and Mother built a new, modern house. He accepted a full time position driving various types of trucks for the Tuscola County Road Commission and was employed there for ten years before he officially retired in 1972 at the age of sixty-five.

Mother and Dad had planted a small garden patch behind the new house shortly after they moved into it. Once he was retired from the road commission, he still had energy to spare, so he expanded the garden to cover a large portion of the three acre plot surrounding the house. Dad spent many happy hours in his "mini-farm", tilling, planting, weeding and harvesting the fruits and vegetables that grew there. The enlarged garden produced far more food than Dad and Mother needed for their own use so he gave the surplus to friends, neighbors and relatives.

Of my three siblings only my sister and I chose to live in Michigan after we were adults. My older brother, Laurel, lived near Seattle in the state of Washington and my younger brother, Dan, lived in New York State near Rochester. About 1980 Mother and Dad, who were in their seventies at the time, decided to pull up stakes in the Vassar area and move closer to Joanne and me. I lived in Midland at the time and she lived near West Branch. They split the difference and, after selling their property near Vassar, bought a

186

home in Gladwin which was between our two communities. That was many years prior to my move to Albuquerque. The house in Gladwin that Mother and Dad purchased came with a couple of acres of land that he almost immediately plowed under and planted to garden. So he was once again back in the business of farming.

My reverie about Dad was interrupted at that point by the flight attendant's announcement that we were about to land at the Tri-Cities Airport serving the Saginaw, Bay City and Midland area of eastern Michigan. Upon landing I retrieved my luggage, picked up my rental car and drove to the nearby motel where I had reserved a room for the week-long stay. I planned to drive to Gladwin the next morning for the dreaded visit with Dad at the nursing home.

Morning dawned bright and clear and by about 10:00 a.m. I pulled into the nursing home parking lot. I recall attempting to boost my spirits as I walked to the entrance by telling myself that perhaps Dad isn't in as bad condition as my fertile imagination was telling me. Maybe he would be having an especially good day. Those periods were rare, according to my sister who saw him regularly, but they did occur.

I arrived at the door of his room and nervously peered in. There he lay in the bed asleep with a sheet covering all but his arms and face. He was a mere shadow of his former robust self. His arms, once so well-muscled, looked like toothpicks. His gaunt, wrinkled face was a pasty gray color and his thin wispy, yellowish hair was in wild disarray. A line of viscous drool led from the lower corner of his lopsided mouth across his chin and was slowly dripping on the sheet below.

Dad awoke soon after I walked into the room. My first thought was, "Will he even know who I am?" From deeply hooded eyes he stared at me with no sign that he recognized me as someone whom he had known intimately for most of his life. He seemed to be asking, "Who is this stranger and what does he want?" Holding his bony, shriveled hand, I vainly attempted to converse with him. I described the weather; I told him about my flight from Albuquerque and also mentioned that I had recently talked on the phone to my sister and both of my brothers. Initially he appeared to be hearing and perhaps even comprehending what I was saying, but in a short time his attention wavered and his eyes glazed over just before he closed them. A gentle snore informed me that the conversation as well as our final visit had come to an end. Devastated, I left the room with hot, salty tears coursing down my cheeks.

Dad died half a year later in February of 2002 when he was a few months short of his ninety-fifth birthday. As I looked at his wasted remains in the coffin I felt grateful that his ordeal was finally over. After a little over five terrible years he had been granted his wish to leave this life.

# CHAPTER 18
# "FITTING IN" IN FOREIGN PLACES

The old adage "Clothing makes the man." certainly is true. A variation on that saying is equally true. That variation is "Clothing makes the foreigner." Though what a person wears will not usually identify exactly what country he hails from, it surely will point out very graphically that he either does or does not fit in where he happens to be at that particular moment in time. Long before the foreigner has even opened his mouth he usually is identified as either being from the local area or being an alien. Then when he speaks the prevalent language with a heavy accent, he only confirms the impression that his clothing has already made.

When I went to Germany as an exchangee in 1953 I packed several pairs of blue jeans in my luggage. As they still are today, jeans were very popular in the United States at that time and were worn by every young person for casual wear. Shorts were almost never worn by teenagers or adults at that time. The only people who were ever seen in public in short pants were young children. In fact there was great pride involved and it was almost ceremonial; when young boys donned their first long pants. In Germany, in the early 1950's, however, the story was far different. For casual wear men, young and old alike, usually wore shorts. The most popular trouser type at the time was the leather shorts, called lederhosen.

Even if a newcomer did wear lederhosen, but they appeared recently purchased, he still was identified as a foreigner. When lederhosen are new they are a gray-green color, but after being well used they become a medium to dark brown. After I bought my first pair I wore them nearly all the time and, because they never are washed or dry cleaned, they soon turned the correct brown shade. I recall that many German men told me that the lederhosen were not really broken in properly until they would stand upright by themselves when they were thrown in a corner. My stay in Germany lasted for a little over five months, and even though I wore them working in the fields they did not become that well broken in. Though my lederhosen never did reach that state, they did help me fit into the German mold much better. Fewer natives stared at me as I went about my daily activities from that point on.

Thirteen years later, in 1966, I made my second trip to the European continent. My American travel agent organized a three-week trip during which I visited some of the major cities in several Western European countries. The trans-Atlantic flight aboard a Scandinavian Air Service (SAS) airplane flew non-stop from New York City to Copenhagen, Denmark. I spent several delightful days there before flying on to Oslo, the capital of Norway, for a short visit. After leaving the Scandinavian Peninsula behind, I visited several different locations in Germany.

During the thirteen year period between 1953 and 1966, clothing styles in the United States changed much. One example of that change was that walking shorts had become very popular as casual wear for men and women. While I was packing my luggage for the trip to Europe I recalled how most German men wore shorts when I was there previously. So, of course, I included several pairs. I felt certain that they would help me fit into the German fashion mold. But I was in for a surprise.

During the thirteen years since I had last stepped foot on German soil much had changed there as well. Most of the buildings which had been destroyed during World War II had been rebuilt and likewise German clothing styles were different from what they had been in 1953. During my two week stay in the country I saw no adult men wearing shorts of any kind—not even lederhosen. That knowledge came as a big shock to me.

Shortly after I flew into West Berlin (it was still divided between the two sectors, East and West, at that time) and was settled in my hotel near the city center, I decided to conduct an experiment. I donned a pair of walking shorts and went for a stroll along the Kurfurstendamm. That was West Berlin's main boulevard where crowds of pedestrians shopped in the fashionable stores that lined its sidewalks. I wanted to observe firsthand the people's reactions to my choice of clothing.

That response was surprisingly swift in manifesting itself. People approaching me on the sidewalk stared so intently that one or two of them nearly walked into lampposts. Once they had passed me, many craned their necks around in order to continue gawking. It didn't take very long to realize that I didn't fit in and that I appeared very alien to the Germans. One stylishly dressed lady pointed at me and whispered loudly to her companion, "Schauen Sie die kurze Hose an! Wie sehr fremd!" ("Look at the short pants! How very strange!") It was obvious to me that she recognized immediately that I was from another country by one of the words she used. "Fremd" in German has at least two definitions. One of the meanings is "strange" but the other meaning is "foreign." She had picked me out to be a foreigner with one quick look at my shorts.

The little experiment didn't last long because I quickly became very self-conscious about being an object of such sartorial curiosity. So, I turned around and ran the gauntlet of staring eyes from there back to my hotel where I changed into long trousers. That ended the wearing of shorts for that particular trip.

While on that same trip I spent a few days in West Berlin with a friend named Kurt who was from Heidelberg. Originally Kurt and I met on my first trip to Germany as an exchangee in 1953. The two of us had been corresponding with another over the years and were pleasantly surprised to learn that we would both be in Berlin at the same time as he was attending a conference there. He promised to show me some of the more interesting tourist attractions of West Berlin during his free time from the conference.

On the first day that we got together to go on a bus excursion around the city, I was wearing a sports jacket. To my way of thinking the jacket was a fairly conservative piece of clothing. It was made of a type of checkered cotton material in several shades of light to very dark gray. Because the design was made up of small checks, my overall impression was that it appeared to be a mottled gray. I was to find out later that my friend did not view the jacket in the same way that I did.

The next morning Kurt had to attend a session at the conference so we made plans to meet at a downtown restaurant for lunch. I went shopping that morning and, among other things, bought a very dark colored suede sports jacket which I was wearing when I arrived at the meeting place. Kurt entered a few minutes later and paused at the door to look for me. I was surprised when he scanned the room a couple of times and overlooked me both times. Finally I motioned toward him and only then did he recognize me and come over to the table.

When out of curiosity I asked why he didn't recognize me immediately; this was his response, "I was looking for that bright checkered sports jacket you were wearing all day yesterday. I didn't even see you because you didn't stand out from the rest of the patrons in the restaurant. The suede jacket makes you fit in perfectly with the natives." Though he was far too polite to say so, I surmised that he had been somewhat embarrassed with my previous day's outfit. My "conservative" sports jacket to his eyes was exactly the opposite and it made me stand out from the crowd. That was yet another piece of clothing that I left folded up in my suitcase for the balance of the trip.

Clothing isn't the only thing that makes one easily distinguishable in a foreign land. Drinking habits and food preferences can be equally as telling. When I was visiting Brittany, France, in 2001, I became aware that not only my inability to speak French, but what I drank (or did not drink) at dinners marked me as an outsider.

Many years ago I stopped drinking alcoholic beverages. I gave them up when the realization came that I simply did not like the way they tasted or the effect they had on me. It doesn't bother me in the least if others in my company wish to drink but I prefer to abstain. That abstinence proved to be difficult in Brittany.

My American traveling companions in France normally ordered wine with their evening meals. Shortly after arriving in the country,

I noticed that most of the menus offered "non-alcoholic" apple cider. Thinking that it might be a good substitute for wine, I tried it and found that it tasted bitter like hard cider does in the United States. That made me suspicious about whether or not it really was a non alcoholic drink even though it was labeled as such. When I questioned the manager of one restaurant about it, he denied over and over again that there was alcohol in his cider. Finally he admitted that all the cider had gone through some fermentation and did contain a little alcohol. I remember the expression of dismay on his face when I explained that I just didn't like the taste of alcohol in drinks and therefore didn't care for wine or hard cider. In France it takes a large amount of chutzpah to state that one dislikes wine. It is much akin to saying in the United States that one hates the flag, Mother, apple pie or baseball. However, from then on I ordered apple juice rather than cider to drink with my meals. It actually did contain no alcohol.

My dislike for the taste of beer once caused me no little embarrassment in Germany and went a long way toward proving to the locals that I didn't fit in well. One of the families I lived with when I was an exchangee in 1953 was the Mayer Family from the tiny agricultural village in Hesse called Lich. The town was well known for its local brewery where Licher Bier was produced. The citizens of Lich were inordinately proud of the native beer and promoted it in every possible way.

In the summer of 1989, my two brothers and I visited the Mayer Family for a couple of days on our driving tour through Europe from England to the southern part of Italy. We arrived at their home in the early afternoon and were greeted enthusiastically by Helmut, his wife and their two sons, Konstatin and Alexander. They insisted that we have refreshments shortly after we arrived so they brought out a variety of cheeses, breads and, of course, the famous Licher Bier. I demurred and mentioned that I wasn't fond of beer. That was a mistake. To say in Germany, especially in a beer producing area of the nation, that one doesn't like beer is tantamount to saying in France that one dislikes wine. It doesn't go over very well. When I saw the looks on my hosts' faces, I realized that I had committed a faux pas of enormous proportions and quickly backtracked. I said that of course I would have a glass of the beer and made a great show of enjoying it thoroughly, even though the exact opposite was the case.

Either the Mayers were convinced by my little charade or they were too civilized to say so because we all had a delightful visit. They demonstrated their usual warm hospitality toward my brothers and me. Helmut and I still correspond with one another upon occasion even though it was fifty-one years ago that I first met him and his family. Very few of my friendships in the United States have lasted nearly that long. However, I still don't fit very well into the German mold, because I continue to dislike the taste of beer!

A person doesn't need to go half way around the world in order to feel that he doesn't fit in with some of the habits of the locals. I moved from the lower peninsula of Michigan to Albuquerque, New Mexico in June of 1997. In most respects, I immediately felt at home upon making the transition. New Mexicans are among the friendliest people I have encountered anywhere in the world. The weather here is extremely pleasant all year round. The summers are hot, but comfortable because of the low humidity and the winters are sunny and mild—especially when compared with those in Michigan. One never seems to run out of interesting sightseeing possibilities in the Southwest either because it is filled with a wide variety of natural and man-made wonders. Carlsbad Caverns, the Jemez Mountains, the Taos Pueblo, the Sandia Mountains, Calle Grande and Chaco Canyon are only a few examples of New Mexico sites that are historically and geographically interesting beyond belief.

A short time after I moved to Albuquerque, I was having lunch in a Mexican style restaurant in the Nob Hill section of Central Avenue. While ordering I asked the waitress for a bowl of chili. What is referred to as chili, in Michigan, is a thick soup-like dish with red beans, onions, meat and tomato sauce. That is what I was expecting. When the waitress served it, I thought that she must have made a mistake and asked her what that green concoction was. She said, "It is chile, like you ordered." Warily, I took a tiny taste of the strange-colored mixture. That one bite nearly blew the top of my head off from its heat! The episode taught me that in the Southwest chile refers to the very hot red or green chile peppers, not the Chili Con Carne that I was accustomed to in the Midwest. If a person here wants the type of chili that I had been served in Michigan, then he must ask for "Texas Chili."

New Mexicans are very fond of their hot chiles. For example they even eat them with their Huevos Rancheros (ranch-style eggs) for breakfast. After a customer orders huevos, the waitperson will immediately ask, "Red, green or Christmas?" Translated that means, "Do you want red chile, green chile or a mixture of the two on your eggs?" The chiles are mixed with a surprising number of other New Mexican dishes such as hamburgers, soups, pizza, candy as well as various types of breads and rolls. In many restaurants most of the entrees will have either red or green chile served on the side or as an integral part of the dish.

As a good example of just how accustomed the natives have become to their hot foods, I'll relate the following true story. A friend of mine who had grown up in Albuquerque and then moved to Denver, Colorado, missed the chile so much that he complained regularly to me in his e-mails and telephone calls. He insisted that he simply couldn't locate a store that sold New Mexico style chile. Feeling very sorry for him, I located a restaurant near the Old Town area that sold bulk items. I sent him a "care package" of a dozen bottles of different chile sauces which he could use when preparing his meals. He was very grateful for the gift.

A number of Mexican-style restaurants here in Albuquerque have a main menu where all the chile-laden entrees are described. Then on another page they will have what is referred to as the "Gringo menu." That part of the menu is for wimps like me whose stomachs can't tolerate hot foods such as green and red chile. "Gringo" is the term used by Hispanics to denote "Americans."

Though I feel very much at home here in the Southwest, I still do not "fit in" well when it comes to the savoring of the region's hot types of foods. Likely in that regard I'll always be an obvious "foreigner."

# CHAPTER 19
# FRUSTRATED IN FRANKFURT

"YOU SIMPLY CAN'T GET THERE FROM HERE!" I screamed internally. That was the frustrated conclusion I came to after attempting to drive from the Frankfurt am Main Airport to the downtown area of the city where my hotel was located. For the past three hours I had been trying desperately to cover the seven miles between the two locations with no success. Normally the trip should have taken about fifteen minutes but, at that point, at least for me, the goal seemed unreachable.

The year was 1966 and I had flown into the Frankfurt Airport from Berlin. Earlier I had reserved a rental car at the airport and planned to spend several days seeing the sights of the city before taking the Autobahn north to the village of Lich where I would visit the Mayer Family with whom I had lived for a time as an exchangee in 1953.

My plane landed on time at the airport and after picking up my luggage, I located the car rental agency desk in the airport concourse. All seemed to be in order because the clerk found my paperwork immediately and soon the Volkswagen's keys were in my hand. I told the clerk that I was going to be staying at the Hotel Continental near the main railroad station. She gave me a map and on it drew the route that I would be taking. Everything seemed to be very straight forward and simple, so I took off with complete confidence that soon I would be checking into the hotel. What actually happened was far different from my expectations.

In a short time after leaving the airport and driving toward the city center, I saw the first sign indicating *Umleitung* (detour). From that point forward, the map the lady had given me was of no use. When I got off the designated route to the hotel I learned that it was impossible to get back on it because of further detours and street closures. Later I discovered the cause for all the traffic disruption was that the city officials were in the middle of a two-year construction project. They were building a subway system to serve the entire urban area of Frankfurt and thus all the major thoroughfares were being torn up. The construction was an enormous undertaking and necessitated rebuilding streets all over the city, resulting in detour after detour.

During the next three hours I drove back and forth across the city in a vain attempt to locate Hebelstrasse, the street on which the Hotel Continental was situated. Each time I thought that I was headed in the correct direction there would be another sign indicating a detour and I would be sent off in a different direction well away from my goal. When finally I was able to locate a street heading in the right direction, it invariably would become a one-way going the wrong way. During that time I must have crossed and re-crossed the Main River a minimum of twenty times without ever finding the correct street. In those three hours I became very familiar with the various bridges leading to and from the downtown area. My frustration level rose to a fever pitch and I feared that there was danger of my having a nervous breakdown right there in the car.

Eventually I noticed a small restaurant on one of the innumerable incorrect streets that I traversed. I pulled the Volkswagen into its parking lot and entered the establishment to have a bite to eat, calm my frazzled nerves and to evaluate my troubled situation. As I ordered the food in my halting German, I also explained the problem to my waiter who, as it happened, owned the restaurant. The man's name was Herr Waldheim and he was most sympathetic. Apparently many of his customers complained about having the same difficulty finding their way around the torn up city. He asked what my destination was and when I told him the Hotel Continental, he smiled and said that he knew exactly where it was and would help me find it. That relieved my mind immensely and consequently I really enjoyed the meal he served me.

After I was finished eating and had paid my bill, Herr Waldheim presented me with a hand-drawn diagram which showed the way to the hotel. On it he even indicated where there were one-way streets and additional detours that might confuse me or send me off in an incorrect direction. After expressing my sincere appreciation, I attempted to tip him, but he was adamant about not accepting any money for merely giving a helpful hand where it was needed. What a good Samaritan he turned out to be! With the aid of his little diagram I was able to drive directly to the Hotel Continental and in less than half an hour I was gratefully turning into its parking lot.

As I parked the car I vowed that I would leave it in the hotel's lot and use public transport until my stay in Frankfurt came to an end. Only when I was leaving three days later for my trip to the village of Lich would I take the rental car out on the detour-filled streets. I had had my fill of stressful attempts to locate the hotel and desired a long respite from it.

Frankfurt is an interesting city with many sightseeing possibilities, most of which are well within walking distance of the Hotel Continental. It took a twenty minute walk or a five minute bus ride to reach the Altstadt, or old city, which forms a half circle on the north bank of the Main River. Remnants of the ancient city walls still stand in the park-like area surrounding the Altstadt on three sides with the river forming the fourth. The ancient church of

St.Bartholomaus dominates its own square and regally sits there in its red-sandstone glory. The church, often misnamed a cathedral, is famous as the site where ten Holy Roman Emperors were crowned.

The historical core of the city is called the Romerberg Platz (Square) and is the site where the Emperor Charlemagne, who pre-dated the Holy Roman Empire, built his fort. In later years, the Romerberg became the market place of old Frankfurt. The residents of the city also take great pride in the fact that the world-renowned writer and poet, Johann Wolfgang von Goethe, was born in the Altstadt sector of Frankfurt. His birthplace is now the Goethe-Haus Historisches Museum and it contains an amazing amount of memorabilia from the Goethe Family possessions.

My days in Frankfurt passed quickly and, though I enjoyed the food, the history of the city and the ebullient spirits of the inhabitants, I dreaded the moment when I would have to get in the car and drive to the Autobahn. From looking at the city map, I learned that the trip was only about four or five miles from my hotel but, if that distance were as difficult to drive as the one from the airport to the hotel, then I was in for a very long and frustrating trip. The day before I was to leave I made a decision which I anticipated would solve the problem.

That morning I arose early and had a good breakfast at the hotel before setting out. I planned to hike the route to the Autobahn and, as I walked, make a diagram of the various streets along the way. I reasoned that using that method, I would know ahead of time where the detours were, which streets were one-way thoroughfares and what the various traffic disruptions were en route to my destination. As it turned out, the ten-mile walk took the largest part of the day but, before I returned to the hotel, I knew all the ins and outs necessary for the next day's drive.

My hike to the Autobahn, though rather long, was a delightful walk through the fashionable and rather expensive West End section of Frankfurt. I passed the Alte Oper (Old Opera House), the Gruneburg Park (Green Castle Park), the Palmen-Garten (an enormous botanical garden and park), and finally the University of Frankfurt. I was in no special hurry and therefore was able to take advantage of and enjoy the interesting sights along the way. Though it was not planned as such, the serendipitous day turned out to be the most enchanting of my time spent in the city.

In the late afternoon I returned to the hotel, tired but secure in my mind that I would be able to drive to the Autobahn the next day with no trouble along the way. A short nap and a hot shower revived me and later I went out for the last evening meal during the visit to Frankfurt.

That night I slept well with no nightmares of endlessly driving back and forth across the Main River in frantic attempts to locate the Autobahn for the trip north to Lich. I awoke refreshed and after breakfasting at the hotel, checked out, and drove out of the hotel parking lot, heading west. Using my hand-drawn diagram and what

I remembered from the previous day's hike, I soon found the on-ramp for the northbound lanes of the Autobahn.

The day was lovely, the traffic was comparatively light and in less than an hour I was pulling into the driveway of the farm home in Lich where I had lived for a time in 1953. Mrs. Mayer warmly greeted me at the door with a hug and a kiss and immediately plied me with coffee and her incomparable pastries. How well I remembered those delicacies from nearly thirteen years ago! She telephoned her son, Helmut, who was studying veterinary science at the nearby Marburg University, and he appeared shortly. We, too, had a boisterous reunion and plied one another with endless questions about how we had fared since last seeing one another. When I first met Helmut he was a teenager in high school. However, by the time of my second visit, he was already married and in his late twenties. Many changes had occurred in his life during the interim.

Helmut also had good news to relate. He and his wife, Helga, had recently been blessed with the birth of their first son, Alexander. Both the mother and baby were doing well and had just come home from the hospital. He was eager for me to accompany him to his home across town in order to meet them.

Over the next few days, the Mayers and I became reacquainted. As they had in 1953, they treated me a part of their family and the intervening years seemed to melt away. I felt equally as comfortable and at home with them as I had when I lived with them over a decade previously.  Our short visit ended much too quickly and then I had to leave the Mayers behind in Lich as I continued on my planned excursion.  In order to catch a plane for Rome, Italy, which was the next stop on my European itinerary, I had to return to the Frankfurt Airport.  Sadly, I bid them goodbye, got in the rental car and headed for the southbound Autobahn.

As it did on my trip north to Lich, the weather proved sunny and warm and I thoroughly enjoyed the picturesque countryside between there and Frankfurt.  The Autobahn route follows a lovely valley on the eastern edge of the Taunus Mountains and along it I passed well known resorts and spas at places like Bad Nauheim, Butzbach and Bad Homburg.  During the drive south I had the forest-covered mountains on my right and on my left was a veritable crazy quilt of odd shaped fields which made up the farms of the region.  Many of the old farm buildings were hundreds of years old, and if one would ignore the super highway on which he was traveling, he could imagine himself transported back to the medieval era.

As I entered the outskirts of Frankfurt, I thought back to the frustrating three hours I had spent trying to drive from the airport to the Hotel Continental.  Though that had been only a week ago, it seemed to me that a very long time had elapsed.  And, I was much relieved that the route of the Autobahn led directly to the Frankfurt Airport and consequently it would be unnecessary to do any additional city driving.  I was far from eager for another "Frustrated in Frankfurt" experience.

# CHAPTER 20
# A TAXI RIDE TO THE GREAT WALL

"You pay this! You pay this!" the taxi driver insisted excitedly as we were ready to enter the parking lot of a museum just outside of the Chinese capital city of Beijing. Before the taxi ride ended late that afternoon, my nephew, Daniel, and I had heard that phrase repeated over and over again until we both were thoroughly exasperated with it and, more to the point, with the man who had been sounding like a broken record for most of the long day.

The two of us had flown from Hong Kong to Beijing the day previous to the taxi ride. That morning at our hotel, the Beijing Hilton, Daniel and I had contracted with the driver and paid for an all day excursion with two major destinations—the Great

Wall of China and the Imperial Summer Palace. The taxi driver conveniently failed to mention that there would be extra costs for us to undertake along the way. Of course, Daniel and I realized that we would have to cover the cost of entrance fees at the tourist stops and for our lunch at a restaurant, but it seemed that the driver fully expected us to fork out additional money wherever we went whether or not there seemed to be any actual need for it.

The above example was a good case in point. On the highway to the Great Wall, just a few miles north of Beijing, the taxi driver asked if we would like to visit an historical museum en route. When we agreed, he pulled into the museum parking lot. We could see no attendant in the lot nor was there a sign demanding a parking fee, yet the driver insisted that we had to pay him to park there. We strongly suspected that the money would go directly into his pocket and would never be given to the museum. Grudgingly we paid the man what he demanded in spite of our misgivings about the situation. That was a decision that would have additional consequences later in the day. By giving in so quickly we convinced the driver that we were "soft touches" and could be easily manipulated into paying for other extras throughout the excursion.

Daniel and I enjoyed our tour through the historical museum. We found it interesting and informative and were pleased that the taxi driver had suggested it despite our suspicions about his motives.

Later we continued on our way north to the Great Wall. Along the way we passed through a small area of rice paddies. That was a surprise because the agricultural area near Beijing is predominantly devoted to wheat production. Most of the usual rice growing areas of China are located in the far southeastern quarter of the country between Shanghai and Canton. Rice crops require a large amount of water and we assumed that the small area of paddies we saw in that region were the result of a rare quirk of nature.

As the miles passed and we distanced ourselves from Beijing, the landscape changed dramatically. The capital city sits on a level sandy plain one hundred miles west of the Gulf of Chihli, an inlet of the Yellow Sea. A few miles out of the city we entered the foothills of the Greater Khingan Mountains and there we were treated to several examples of traditional Chinese architecture in the form of pagodas. Pagodas are eight sided temples or memorials common in Asia. Those in China are made of brick, glazed tile or porcelain. They are built so that each succeeding story is slightly smaller than the one on which it rests. The tower-like structures feature wide, highly decorated and upward curving roof overhangs above each level. Often the pagodas nestle among the hills and fit artistically into the tree-covered natural landscape.

From the windows of the taxi we could see the mountains rising to extreme elevations just north of us. In those heights the early Chinese people built the Great Wall to protect themselves from invasions of the war-like Tartars from the Mongolian Empire which lay across the border. We were able to catch occasional glimpses of the huge protective wall as it undulated across the mountains and through the green valleys in the distance.

Eventually we stopped at a small settlement lying adjacent to the south side of the Great Wall. The Chinese as well as people from the rest of the world are drawn in great numbers to the renowned structure, so it has developed into a popular tourist attraction. Thousands of people travel there daily in order to walk atop the ramparts and examine the battlements along a small portion of its length. The settlement next to the wall provided tourist accommodations and housed the government workers who manage the business end of the sightseeing enterprise. Anyone could see that the area fairly bristled with official looking uniformed officers who were well armed. I was unaware of it at the time but we were shortly destined to run afoul of some of those officials.

Near a sign marked "ENTRANCE TO THE GREAT WALL," the taxi driver pulled into an open area that seemed vacant. He totally ignored another sign at the entrance from the street, which we learned later, stated that the area was for official use only and stopping there by anyone else was strictly prohibited. Before we could open the doors to get out, the car was surrounded by a half dozen officers with rifles in their hands. Their leader officiously approached the taxi driver and a lengthy conversation ensued with much yelling and many gesticulations on both their parts. Daniel and I were completely at a loss to know what was happening but we were aware that whatever it was, it was not good!

When the harangue quieted down, the driver turned and informed us we were stopped in an illegal area and the officer was demanding the immediate payment of a fine for the infraction. Then came the bombshell. The driver expected Daniel and me to pay the penalty in spite of the fact that he had been the one who ignored the sign and thus broke the law!. We of course adamantly refused. We had already been disillusioned with his charging us for the parking fee at the museum lot with no assurance of its legitimacy and now he expected us to come across with payment for his transgression. At that point we stopped talking to him altogether. He turned around in the seat and implored us. "You pay! You pay!" was his oft repeated refrain. We both looked away and ignored him. The stalemate lasted for about ten minutes during which the driver talked earnestly with first one of us and then the other in a vain attempt to divide and conquer. We gave him the cold shoulder through it all and refused to respond to his pleas.

Meanwhile the official resolutely insisted on the payment and the armed guards continued to surround the taxi. Their rifles were not pointing at us but they were in their hands ready for use at any moment. At last we realized that we had won the contest of wills when the driver reached into his pocket, pulled out his wallet and gave the officer some bills. The official went away satisfied, the guards retreated and we drove out of the forbidden area and located a parking place nearby. The driver did not attempt to extract further money from us for parking there. We hoped that he had learned a lesson.

The driver remained with the taxi while Daniel and I spent a couple of hours examining the man-made wonder that is the Great Wall of China. The enormous structure is about 1,500 miles long and meanders across much of the northern portion of the country in a generally east-west direction. It was under construction at various times from as early as 221 B.C. until 1644 A.D. The section that we examined was about twenty-five feet high with a brick-paved flat top, roughly fifteen feet wide, on which mounted sentinels patrolled in days gone by. Along its length there were taller guard towers built at intervals of from two hundred to three hundred feet. The wall follows an erratic course as it meanders up and down and here and there across the rough terrain. Portions of it are visible as it scales the peaks far off in the distance to the east and to the west. From the wall the views of the surrounding verdant mountains are spectacular and we snapped dozens of photographs as we made our way along the crowded roadway atop the wall. The day was beautifully clear and sunny therefore hundreds of tourists were out enjoying the summer weather and the view from the ancient marvel.

A few years ago the story was widely circulated that the Great Wall of China is the only man-made structure large enough to be seen by astronauts from space. Later the story was proven to be a figment of some person's vivid imagination because the National Aeronautics and Space Administration (NASA) officials denied its veracity. It matters little whether or not the wall may be seen from outer space because it is spectacularly impressive when viewed from here on Earth.

After our curiosity about the wall was satisfied, we rejoined the taxi driver for the trip back to Beijing where we were to visit the Imperial Summer Palace in a suburb near there. However, before reaching that destination we were about to experience yet another taste of the driver's economic chicanery.

A few miles along the route south toward Beijing, the driver innocently asked if we would like to stop for lunch. Daniel and I hadn't eaten since breakfast so we readily agreed. During the next half hour or so the driver passed up several restaurants along our route before he pulled into the driveway of a small building on the verge of the highway. There were no evident signs indicating that it was a restaurant; in fact it appeared to be merely a private home. No sooner had the taxi come to a halt in the driveway, than the front door burst open. A man rushed out and greeted us with great enthusiasm. It was obvious to us that he knew our taxi driver well and was expecting our arrival. The gregarious host invited all of us into the home and soon we were seated around the table in his dining room.

The owner explained what his little establishment was capable of preparing for our meal. He described a sumptuous feast that far exceeded our expectations of a simple lunch and then sat back with greedy eyes gleaming, to note our response. My nephew, Daniel, who spoke enough Mandarin to make himself understood, asked him what the meal would cost. When he heard the answer Daniel turned to me and exclaimed that the price was exorbitant—in fact, much more than we were accustomed to paying for fine meals in the fancy restaurants in Hong Kong. The host obviously felt that he had a captive clientele and that this would be a financial bonanza for him. We conferred between ourselves and agreed that the cost was far too much. Daniel, in his halting Mandarin, managed to convey to the host that we had no desire for a huge feast and, instead, would like a light lunch of some sort of egg and rice combination. With his disappointment over a lost opportunity plainly evident, the host suggested what Daniel felt was a reasonable price for the simpler fare. We agreed to it and he morosely went off to the kitchen to prepare it.

As the three of us were waiting for lunch, the taxi driver, during his conversation, inadvertently let it slip that he and the establishment's host were related. Almost immediately he turned a bright shade of crimson upon realizing what he had just admitted. "Oho!" we thought! The entire plot suddenly became very clear to us. No wonder we had passed right by the restaurants along the highway and instead had stopped for lunch at this private home. Of course! The taxi driver was in league with the owner of the establishment and would be receiving a kickback from him for bringing us there to eat. It was just one more way for him to make money off the "rich" tourists. At that point I silently congratulated

Daniel for insisting that our lunch be a less expensive one rather than what had been originally suggested by our host.

When the food was placed on the table, it was plain but tasty fare exactly as we had anticipated. I noticed that that taxi driver liberally helped himself which was fine with us as he too had to eat. Afterward, however, while Daniel and I paid the bill, he managed to be well occupied in another part of the room and didn't offer to contribute anything for his share of the lunch. By that time we were not in the least surprised at such antics on his part. He had already convinced us that he was an unscrupulous creature with little or no conscience or sense of fair play.

After lunch we resumed out trip south to the ancient Summer Palace of the Chinese emperors. The palace is an enormous dwelling situated beside a large lake on the outskirts of Beijing. The taxi pulled into the parking lot just outside the gate to the palace and stopped there. The driver rather brusquely told us that the stay was only going to be a short one and that we were to be back at the parking lot in one hour's time. As Daniel and I walked through the massive gates toward the palace proper, we discussed the driver and his ultimatum. We knew from what we could see of the multi-storied structure in the distance that we could never do the visit any sort of justice in only an hour. Therefore, we decided that because we had rented the taxi and driver for the entire day and the price included visits to <u>both</u> the Great Wall and the Summer Palace, we would ignore his demand and take whatever time we deemed necessary to see it adequately.

Unhurriedly we explored the lush gardens, colorful courtyards and opulent rooms of the luxurious villa and from its lofty verandas drank in picturesque views of the lake. We also walked along the edge of the water and later boarded the imperial yacht. Apparently the emperor who had it built either was fearful of seasickness or had no interest in sailing, because the vessel was constructed entirely of stone and thus was unable to move from its permanent mooring site. Visitors to the yacht walked across a stone ramp that connected it to the pier.

A little under two hours later we headed back to the parking lot at the palace entrance. There we were met by the taxi driver who was livid! Over and over again he pointed at his wristwatch and yelled, "I say one hour, no two hour!" Daniel and I pretended that we had no inkling about what he was screaming and ignored him completely. We had not been told of any deadline for returning to the hotel from the day's excursion so we couldn't understand why he wanted to cut our visit to the Summer Palace so short. Besides that, we felt that he had taken advantage of us, or at least attempted to do so, enough times that day that he deserved being thwarted in returning exactly when he wished to. Revenge can be very sweet, indeed.

# CHAPTER 21
# A MEMORABLE VISIT TO
# NORTHERN FRANCE

In early September during the fall of 2001, several friends and I spent a few weeks in France. Because various members of the party were arriving from several different locations, we all met at the Charles de Gaulle Airport which serves the greater Paris area. There we picked up our rental car and began a leisurely three-day trip from the capital city to our eventual destination of Trigavou, a rustic village in northern Brittany.

The first day we visited the extensive estate and gardens of the renowned Impressionist painter, Claude Monet, in the rural hamlet of Giverny about forty-five miles northwest of Paris. Monet moved there in 1883 with his two sons, his mistress and her six children.

He resided there for the last forty-three years of his life. The artist's pink two-story mansion with green shutters sits on verdant, plant-filled grounds with undulating paths throughout the area. The entire estate, with its Japanese inspired lily ponds and its colorful, kaleidoscopic blooms have all been lovingly restored to Monet's own designs. It truly displays his passion for vivid color. A tour of the gardens is like taking a walk through a three dimensional, Impressionist painting by the artist.

The following day we drove forty miles northeast to Amiens, on the River Somme, to view the largest Gothic cathedral in all of France. Like its counterpart in Paris, it is called the Cathedral of Notre Dame, but this structure is twice as large and dominates an enormous square in the center of Amiens, a city of a little over a hundred thousand residents. The giant house of worship was built during the first half of the Thirteenth Century and, unlike most Gothic cathedrals, was completed in less than fifty years from the time construction was begun. Along with many other tourists, we admired the delicate front façade with its twin bell towers, reminiscent of the Reims Cathedral. Literally hundreds of intricately carved figures, each set in its own stone niche, decorated the arched entrances. Through twenty foot tall wooden doors we entered the dim interior and walked down the center aisle of the nave toward the opulent altar in front. Our combined footsteps echoed eerily in the exalted heights of the cathedral's interior. As we turned from the altar our eyes were drawn upward to the lacy, colorful rose window set in the wall over the main entrance. I am not a religious person by nature, but even I felt a distinct sense of spirituality in the hushed interior of the towering edifice.

On the third day out from Paris we drove into Trigavou. The village lies about seven miles south of Saint-Malo, a small city on an inlet of the English Channel. Trigavou is a quaint hamlet on the rolling French coastal plain. It features narrow, winding streets, a small medieval-looking business district, tall green hedges, prodigious vegetable and flower gardens, a beautiful slate-roofed church, walled courtyards and ancient houses with many interesting outbuildings.

Our headquarters for the two week visit was a large two and a half story house on the edge of the village which we had rented for the duration of our stay. The main house was built of tan, beige and rust colored stone and the doors and window sashes were painted a light blue. Colorful flower boxes graced the first floor window sills. The walls of the house were three feet thick and there was a graveled courtyard in front for parking. At the rear there was a small orchard surrounding a wooden chicken coop housing a dozen or so laying hens. During our stay we had the added advantage of being able to use fresh eggs from the small flock of chickens.

Inside the house, the entire first floor was made up of one large room used as kitchen, dining room and living room. A wood-burning fireplace was centered on a long, stone wall of the living area. Heavy, rough-hewn beams decorated the low ceiling and a circular dark-stained wooden stairway at the back of the room wound its way to the upper two floors where there were two bathrooms and five bedrooms.

The structure on the property which I found most interesting however, was one of the outbuildings. At the outer edge of the front courtyard near the wall was a miniature stone building currently being used as a workshop, though it appeared originally to have been built as a stable for small animals such as ponies. The second floor contained a loft area where hay had been stored and was reached by double doors located in a narrow central gable over the front door. A couple of tiny, symmetrical windows, set high in the wall of the first floor, framed the front door. Across one end there was a lean-to addition also built of stone with a slanted roof. Like the main house, the little outbuilding was adorned by a slate roof and all its doors and window sashes were painted light blue. The structure was utterly charming. All of us took photographs of the quaint building and one of our companions, an accomplished artist, also painted several water colors of it.

Over the next two weeks we made forays to various tourist attractions in the provinces of Brittany and neighboring Normandy. We visited the French version of the English Stonehenge at Carnac on the Atlantic Ocean coast. The megaliths there, reputedly set in place by the ancient Druids, seemingly march in strict formations and cover miles of the rolling country side overlooking the ocean shoreline. One of the huge stones was particularly noteworthy as it protruded from the ground, rose about twenty feet in the air and had a radius of approximately eight or nine feet. The real mystery, as at Stonehenge in England, is how were the stones, each weighing many tons, hauled to the location and set in place prior to the invention of the wheel?

We took another side trip about thirty-five miles northeast of Trigavou, just off the English Channel coast, to the abbey of Mont-Saint-Michel. That mass of granite protruding 264 feet from the channel waters is connected to the mainland by sand bars during low tide but becomes an island during high tide. One of the most popular tourist attractions in France, Mont-Saint-Michel hosts throngs of visitors, particularly during the summer months.

To reach the combination Romanesque and Gothic style abbey, which is perched high atop the island, tourists must walk through the steeply ascending streets of the village of Mont-Saint-Michel at its base. From the main entrance it is a further climb up nine hundred steps to attain the highest level of the abbey. While taking the tour, one walks through a maze of spacious rooms, stairways, vaulted halls, grassy terraces and arched cloisters. From atop the abbey, we observed the blue waters of the channel on one side and the lush rural mainland of Brittany on the other. The views were superb.

Mont-Saint-Michel was under construction for over five hundred years and the stone used for building was laboriously hauled there from nearby islands in the English Channel. I was particularly fascinated by their method for transporting building materials and supplies to the abbey's heights. Inside the lowest level of the structure (but still hundreds of feet above the water line) was a giant wheel about thirty feet in diameter and three feet from side to side. A heavy rope wound around its protruding axle and was attached through an opening in the wall to a sled-like cart that ran along a nearly-vertical ramp down the steep incline. The items to be raised on this crude elevator were strapped or tied to the sled which was pulled to the top by the rope. But, what powered the huge wheel, I wondered. The guide explained to us that men walked inside the wheel making it turn, causing the rope to wind around the axle and therefore raising the sled. Somewhat like an oversized exercise wheel for gerbils. Crude but effective, I thought.

In its long history Mont-Saint-Michel has been a church, a monastery, an abbey and even a governmental prison for a time. During the Hundred Years' War, when that part of Brittany was under the control of the English, the abbey served as a haven for French pilgrims who came there for safety from the invaders. At present it is maintained by the government and a few monks live and worship in its expansive interior.

One of my overwhelming reasons for the trip to northern France was to visit the Utah and Omaha Beaches in Normandy—the neighboring province to the east from Brittany. On June 6, 1944 (D-Day) the Allied invasion of Nazi-occupied Europe began there. My father's youngest brother, Uncle Melvin, was an American sailor who took part in the invasion and was lost at sea when his ship sank in the English Channel off the Normandy coast. My brother, Dan, visited the sight a few years earlier and told me that there was a memorial to Uncle Melvin in the American Cemetery there and I was eager to see it and the place where he lost his life.

At Point du Hoc, a part of Omaha Beach, I walked across the nearly white sand and looked to the bluffs behind with their cannon and machine gun emplacements that Allied invaders faced during the attack. After observing the remains of the cement bunkers, blockhouses and machine gun nests that formed part of the German-built defensive perimeter of Europe, I wondered how any of the attackers could have survived. To do so it was necessary for them to cross the broad beach and scale the bluffs in the face of withering fire from the entrenched German in their fortifications at the crest. It took little imagination to conjure up the horror of war and the fear that each of the allied soldiers must have felt on that fateful morning.

Further along the rugged and windswept beach toward the east I visited the beautiful Monument to the Normandy Landings. The memorial was erected and is maintained by the American government on land donated to the United States for that purpose by the grateful French government. I climbed the stairs to the top of the monument and from that vantage point took in the dramatic view of the sandy beaches and the still-present wreckage of invasion craft rising above the shallow blue waters that presently are so peaceful.

On a lovely hilltop near the village of Colleville-sur-Mer stands the American Cemetery and Memorial. It is a moving tribute to the thousands of fallen servicemen who gave their lives in the Allied cause against the Axis powers. There are avenues of hundreds of Holly Oak trees which are pruned in the shapes of open parachutes. In the cemetery nearly a thousand tombstones made of white marble honor those whose bodies were recovered. Members of the Jewish faith are commemorated by a Star of David and all others by a Latin cross. They form precise rows in the closely cropped lawn areas. From the cemetery there is a commanding view across the English Channel to the north.

At the cemetery visitors' center I inquired about where my uncle's commemoration could be found. The attendant looked up his name on a computer and gave me a printout. On the sheet was all of the documented information about him that the government has in its death registry. It listed his full name, rank, serial number, military unit, state in which he was born, his military decorations and finally, his official date of death. I later learned that the date of death was determined by a formula. The government decided that the official death date would be one year and one day after the serviceman was listed as missing in action. Uncle Melvin's date of death was June 20, 1945, so he was missing in action on June 19, 1944. The attendant explained to me that because his body was never recovered from the sea, Uncle Melvin's name could be found carved in the Wall of the Missing. He gave me directions to the

Memorial and indicated that the Wall was in the gardens directly behind it.

After a short walk I located the Memorial which is a colonnade built of white marble in a half circle. In the center of the arc formed by the columns is a twenty-two foot bronze statue called "The Spirit of American Youth Rising from the Waves." The statue was carved by a man named Donald De Lue from New Jersey. I walked past the statue and down the short stair leading to the symmetrical gardens in back. They, too, were in a half circle and were ringed by the curving Wall of the Missing. Engraved on the salmon-colored marble wall are 1,557 names, but I had no problem locating the one I was interested in seeing: "MELVIN L. DAVIS." Though it was a warm September day, I felt a chill sweep cross my body and tears traced their way down my cheek as I paid my last respects to a kinsman who had sacrificed his life for his country.

My short visit to northern France embraced many noteworthy events all of which were interesting and gratifying. However, I must confess that none was more memorable than the visit to the Normandy coast. Monet's beautiful estate, the colossal megaliths at Carnac, and even awe-inspiring Mont-Saint-Michel pale into insignificance when compared with that. Seeing the D-Day Invasion site and Uncle Melvin's name on the Wall of the Missing were memories I shall always treasure.

# EPILOGUE

Travel has been one of my overriding interests since I was an elementary pupil at a two-room school in the village of Tuscola, Michigan, during the late 1930s. I recall a shelf on one side of our classroom where a sizeable collection of *National Geographic* magazines resided and I spent many fascinating hours pouring over those fonts of information. The articles and photographs they contained gave me my first glimpses of such foreign places as Europe, Africa and the Orient. The images gained at that young age set my imagination afire and once I learned that alien places existed I was eager to enlarge my personal world by experiencing them myself.

I was particularly taken with pictures and stories depicting the wide variety of exotic architecture from various parts of the world. Medieval castles, ancient pyramids, inspiring cathedrals, grandiose mansions, picturesque Alpine chalets, Oriental pagodas and even crude thatched huts dotted the colorful pages and stimulated my interest. I eagerly looked forward to the day when I would have the opportunity to walk in the same rooms where knights, popes, tycoons, emperors and kings had spent their time. That was heady stuff for a seven or eight year old boy from rural Michigan who, at that point, had traveled no more than seventy-five miles from the farmhouse where he was born.

Certain problems, though, do arise when one does any amount of traveling around our planet. The most obvious of those is language. Though not being able to speak the native language when in a foreign country is a problem, it does not need to become an insurmountable obstacle. I have learned that I can get most, if not all, of my ideas across to locals by a combination of hand and head gestures in combination with facial expressions. In addition, I usually carry a small dictionary containing both English and the local language, and in case I find the word I want is, for me, unpronounceable, then I merely point it out to the person to whom I'm speaking. Most people I've come into contact with around the world have been very welcoming and they usually go out of their way to be helpful.

A second problem worth mentioning which predominantly affects travelers who go on trips by themselves, is loneliness. Some people find it devastating to spend a few weeks in a strange environment where they don't understand the language and have no familiar companions nearby. For those people the obvious solution is to travel in organized tours, of which there are many. The tour director takes care of the all travel arrangements, thus solving the language barrier, and other members of the group provide the needed companionship. I have never been aversely affected by traveling alone. In fact, in 1966 I spent three weeks in Europe by myself and visited Denmark, Norway, East and West Germany, Italy and

England. I had a wonderful time and met many, many interesting people simply because I was forced to do so.

A third problem facing travelers is currency. A case in point is the following: Prior to the introduction of the *Euro* each European country had its own separate currency. Of course, that meant that every time one crossed a national border, the monetary system changed. My solution for that was simple. Before leaving the United States I would buy small amounts of each of the currencies of the countries I planned to visit and put them in separate, marked envelopes. And, in each envelope I would place a small, self-made chart with examples of dollars with their equivalents in the foreign currency. For example: $1.00 = 4.00 Deutsch Marks, $10.00 = 2.00 Pounds Sterling, or $5.00 = 2,000.00 Italian Lira, et cetera. Therefore when I looked at prices in the various countries I could refer to the appropriate chart of dollar equivalents and know almost immediately whether or not I could afford the item. Doing that small amount of preparation ahead of time saved me much confusion while in the foreign country and made the various currencies easier to deal with.

During the past fifty years I have traveled thousands of miles but there still are many places that remain on my "to visit" list. One of the first of those which comes to mind immediately is the Opera House in Sydney, Australia. Amazingly that futuristic-looking structure was built when I was still a child, and I remember reading an article in the *Reader's Digest* about the difficulties encountered during its construction. The opera house's unusual shape—resembling billowing sails—captured my childish imagination and still fascinates me today.

Numbered among the other noteworthy and interesting sites I still wish to visit are The Acropolis in Athens, Greece, the Pyramids of Giza in Egypt, the newly-built capital of Brazil (called Brasilia), the ancient Incan ruins at Machu Pichu in Peru, the fjords of New Zealand, in addition to the cities of Moscow and St. Petersburg in Russia. With any luck at all, traveling to those locations should provide me with stories enough to fill *Tales of the Road, Volume II.*

# ABOUT THE AUTHOR

Jerry Davis holds bachelor's and master's degrees in history from Michigan universities. He taught junior high school history and geography in Michigan schools and retired in 1986 after a 31 year career in education. Since 1997, Jerry has resided in Albuquerque, New Mexico where he is a member of SouthWest Writers (SSW) an organization of New Mexico authors. Jerry's first book, *Home on the Farm: Essays on a Michigan Childhood,* was published in October of 2003. He is a freelance writer whose articles have appeared in newsletters, newspapers and magazines. The November, 2003 issue of *The Good Old Days* magazine contained one of Jerry's articles called, "The Mouths of Babes."

Printed in the United States
25242LVS00001B/163-174

9 781418 487195